COPY 71 94

Biography Broun, Heywood Hale, 1918-
Broun   Whose little boy are you? : a memoir
         of the Broun family / by Heywood Hale
         Broun. -- New York : St. Martin's/Ma-
         rek, 1983.

         215 p.

         ISBN 0-312-87765-X : $14.95

         1.Broun, Heywood Hale, 1918-
         2.Broun, Heywood, 1888-1939--Biography.
         3.Hale, Ruth, 1887-1934.

Redford Township Library   7657   Ap83
    15150 Norborne
Detroit, Mich. 48239
    531-5960   83-3277
            CB CARD CORPORATION OF AMERICA   AACR2   CIP MARC   9

Whose Little
Boy Are
You?

Whose Little Boy Are You?

∘∘

A Memoir
of the
Broun
Family

∘∘

Heywood
Hale
Broun

St. Martin's/Marek

Design by Andy Carpenter

Library of Congress Cataloging in Publication Data

Broun, Heywood Hale, 1918–
  Whose little boy are you?

    1. Broun, Heywood Hale, 1918–   . 2. Broun, Heywood, 1888–1939
—Biography.   3. Hale, Ruth, 1887–1934.   4. Authors, American—20th
century—Biography.   5. Journalists—United States—Biography.   I. Title.
PN4874.B76A34   1983   070'.92'4 [B]   83-3277
ISBN 0–312–87765–X

First Edition
10 9 8 7 6 5 4 3 2 1

For Mattie Wilson Simmons
Who Loved Us All

Whose Little Boy Are You?

●

In the early 1960s I was rehearsing a television show in which I had the role of a juiceless, joyless teacher in a high school high-jinks comedy. During a coffee break one of the teenaged actors, finding something vaguely familiar about my name, asked whether my father had been an actor too.

"My God, I feel old," said the director. "He doesn't know who Heywood Broun was!"

"I feel good," I said, but, of course, I didn't, really. The children of the famous may resent the shadow in which they dwell, but when and if it disappears, they know sadly that parent has died for a second time.

I was at this time a moderately successful actor, a veteran of a dozen Broadway shows and perhaps 150 television dramas. I had also been a newspaperman, a soldier, and a partner in a small jazz record company. I wasn't exactly sure what I wanted to be but I knew what I wasn't. I wasn't Heywood Broun. I knew this because people being introduced to me were always saying, "Heywood Broun, Heywood Broun? You can't be Heywood Broun. You're too young to be Heywood Broun. He was a big man, black curly hair. I'll never forget him."

My explanation used to begin, "Well, I am and I'm not," and from there on would be ruefully comic, charmingly wistful, or short and irritable depending on my current feelings.

When the young man asked whether my father had been an actor, I realized that for some time the number of people who jibbed at my introduction had been shrinking. Certainly few people who grabbed me by the hand said, "Heywood Broun, Heywood Broun, love you on the *Mr. Peepers Show*," but there was no doubt the shadow was beginning to fade, and I felt unfairly uneasy.

I had spent much of my life being angry at Heywood for all the reasons sons have for being mad at their fathers with a few extra ones special to us thrown in, but I never forgot for a moment that he was a *great man*. I never forgot, even as I raged at her, that my mother, Ruth Hale, was a *great woman*, even though her public recognition was, after a time, less than his.

I didn't want them to be forgotten, and in telling my friends about their oddities and inadequacies as parents, I always managed to alternate my whimperings with boasts of their many accomplishments.

Being both resentful and reverential is hard work, and I used to fantasize about what ideal parents would be, deciding at last that a boy would be lucky if his father were the second-best shoemaker in a medium-sized town. No one would then say to him, "You'll never be able to make a pair of reverse calf Romeos like your dad, kid. You better just stick to half soles and heels." Neither, of course, would you be the shamefaced bearer of messages to the old man about repairs that split open within a week.

The town, just big enough to make his rank meaningful— there had to be more than just three cobblers—would be comfortable, and wonderfully compatible groups of kids would always be gathering on each other's big front porches. Even in this daydream of comfort through mediocrity, however, I didn't want my mother appearing on that porch with a plate of cookies. I shared enough of Ruth's feminism to want the shoemaker's wife to be an intellectual, smarter than her husband perhaps, as Ruth was basically smarter than Heywood, but I wanted her to be always ready with a good supply of that essential juvenile nourishment, reassurance.

It's a sad little dream and no pair was farther from Ma and Pa Shoesters than Ruth and Heywood. To begin with, neither of them was second best.

Almost from the beginning Heywood was a vast success in the newspaper business. In his day he was straight reporter, war correspondent, sports writer, drama critic, book critic, and general columnist. If some people did one of those things better than he did, no one could match him at all of them. And yet at the peak of his career he risked the anger of his employers, an anger that eventually destroyed that career, in order to be among the principal founders of the American Newspaper Guild, and its first president, a job he held while he lived.

He was philanthropical, incorruptible, and colorful. Ten thousand people went to his funeral.

When I felt resentful about unsatisfactory aspects of our relationship, some of these awesome facts would fall on me like stones, and I would wonder how a little, boil-covered, ill-favored, general disappointment like myself dared to resent anyone like that. Still, I went on resenting.

As to the reassurance I was hoping for, Ruth thought that sort of thing was the camomile tea of cowards, and in her endless, honorable, never-victorious battle against an unfair world she neither brewed it nor drank it, although I think a cup now and then would have done us both a world of good.

Despite a narrow small-town education, she was the best-informed person in matters pertaining to the arts that I ever met. After a distinguished stretch of years as a writer for newspapers and magazines, she became, after her work seemed to her to be derailed by marriage, a fighter for many causes. She was the co-founder and first president of the Lucy Stone League, a group of women who kept their own names. You can find her in many old law books as a plaintiff against the State Department in her unsuccessful battle to get a passport as herself and not as somebody's wife.

She was secretary of the League to Abolish Capital Punishment, and, unyielding on matters great or small, once drove an exhausting, late-night, extra hundred miles to avoid sleeping in the town where lived the judge who had sentenced Sacco and Vanzetti.

It would not be fair to say she never gave me comfort and reassurance. It's just that she was better at bugle calls than lullabies and made her largest contributions in the form of pushes toward an ideal made magnificent by the fact that it was unattainable. She wanted me to be a free soul who never broke any rules.

Measuring them against the shoemaker scale of parental success, Ruth and Heywood probably would come at the top of the bottom third of the sampling, although if you weighted the statistics with an effort factor they would move up the scale—even though some of the efforts were strange and silly.

Neither of them lived to see how I turned out, and I later made out of their presumed dismay quite a nice, wry party monologue. Self-denigration, when skillfully done, is a great attention getter, and my well-rehearsed stories of defeat and discomfiture filled, if not theaters, at least living rooms with laughter. I was often praised for my modesty, but looking back I realize that I carried modesty over the border and into the realm of self-abasement.

The great actor-director Louis Jouvet once said that anyone could deal with failure. Billions did it every day, few of them realizing how hard it would be to deal with success.

Bumping comfortably along in my good-sport goat cart—"If I tell you the name of my part, 'The Second Bank Clerk,' it'll give you some idea of its scope. . . . The day they put my name on the side of the delivery trucks the newspaper folded up. . . . I am either a Renaissance man or one who has failed in a remarkable variety of professions. . . . My mother and father came back to this country so I could be born here and therefore eligible for the presidency of the United States. It's one of the many ways in which I disappointed them. . . ."—I used to quote Jouvet but I didn't, and couldn't, understand what he meant.

In 1968, sitting in a room at the Ritz Hotel in Boston, drinking whiskey out of a tooth glass and crying while sipping, I began to get his drift. I was now, at last, a Success.

A year older than Ruth when she died, two years older than Heywood when he died, I was playing a leading role in a play bound for Broadway, had recently become a well-known television news correspondent, and had written a critically successful book. In the Snakes and Ladders game of celebrity, I was competing with them, and was suddenly uncertain as to whether, in those ghostly chambers of my head and heart from which they gave advice, they were pleased to have me in the game.

The play went to New York and to a failure that the author said was due to the laugh-oriented insensitivity of the actors, and I sought the comfort of psychotherapy.

Making it a lot shorter than I did for the doctor, the result after four years was that I felt better about myself and better about them, even as I realized with a pang that there were signs of packing up in the ghostly chambers.

If I think of them less often now, I think of them when I do with less awe, more amusement, less anger, more affection. We are now three old people who are rather comfortable together. We are not three old saints, and there are still scars that throb on cold and miserable days, and there are some regrets that will last as long as I do.

Since I may be packing soon myself, however, I wanted to put down and make some shape of what I remember about three exasperating, interesting people who seemed to spend a lot of time slamming doors on each other and then opening them to cry out "Where are you? I need you!" Door slamming days are over because only one of us is left. Whether I have opened the right doors in the mazy corridors of recall, I don't

•

know, but anyway here we are, the cast in order of appearance —Ruth Hale, Heywood Broun, and Heywood Hale Broun.

•   •

When Heywood Broun and Ruth Hale were married on June 7, 1917, the best man, Franklin P. Adams, called them "the clinging oak and the sturdy vine." Certainly this seemed a fair description to those who had attended the wedding, a power struggle between the bride and the groom's mother that everybody, much later, decided should be treated as an amusing and colorful occasion.

Ruth had wanted a ceremony as bare of ritual as possible, a quick trip to city hall with a couple of friends as witnesses. Mrs. Heywood Cox Broun wanted her favorite child to have a proper Episcopal church wedding, and Heywood just wanted to get married without making anybody angry.

Uncharacteristically, Ruth gave way to Mrs. Broun, but characteristically insisted on considerably altering the normal arrangements. To begin with, there was to be "No goddamned music—no marching down the aisle to Mendelssohn." Heywood's mother pretended to agree to this, but, not a woman to be balked, arranged for the hiring of an organist.

When this artist began rolling out his triumphant chords, Mrs. Broun smiled with satisfaction, Heywood turned pale, and nothing else happened. Midway through a second chorus, a messenger tiptoed down the side aisle to tell Mrs. Broun that Miss Hale was not entering until the music stopped. Mrs. Broun tested this resolve through another interminable repetition before sending the messenger to the organ loft with the word of surrender. In mid-bar the church was suddenly, eerily, silent and Ruth Hale came sternly down the aisle.

A whole deceptive pattern was set up at that moment, the pattern of the clinging oak and the sturdy vine, a pattern as boldly obvious as a Pre-Raphaelite story painting, but a pattern that like the picture had a complex and contrapuntal understructure.

The bride's walk was brisk and firm, quite unlike the trance-like glide appropriate to the ritardando rhythms of "The Wedding March." It was the purposeful tread of the crusader as she marched toward the passive, perspiring man who was distributing placatory smiles to everyone in view.

Ruth felt that the musical betrayal was just another proof that compromise was disastrous. By agreeing to show up at a foolish place to go through an outmoded ritual, she had led the enemy to doubt her resolution.

Still, for all the purposeful pace and the unbending resolution, Ruth Hale was terrified as later she was to be terrified by the idea of motherhood. In both cases she did the same thing —put on a stainless steel face, impervious enough to keep the most corrosive of her fears from leaking out.

Telling the story of the wedding was one of the features of her fund of anecdotes. Heywood, who had stood mutely neutral through the whole battle of wills between his mother and his bride, used to stand similarly mute during the telling of the story and never, in my hearing, commented on it or corrected it.

As Ruth told it, she trumpeted the responses to an edited version of the service that, in another insisted-upon change, left out the "obey" business, while Heywood mumbled his. Frank Adams was spared the best man's traditional fumble for the ring because there wasn't any.

Heywood's fears were more obvious, but fright was so often running, spike-shod, through his insides that he probably didn't notice that this day wasn't very different from all the others on which he did things that displeased those apparently perfect people, Heywood Cox Broun and Henrietta Brosé Broun.

On the face of things, this is all pretty Strindbergian, but the marriage of my parents was in its many paradoxes and intellectual poses closer to the work of Shaw or Wilde.

I never heard much about Ruth's father, a gentle man who seemed to have wearied early of the fears that life on the anxious edge of gentility imposed. I was never told what he died of, knowing only that given the choice of Rogersville, Tennessee, or the grave, he hadn't much difficulty in deciding.

It's easy to say from the superficial evidence of obvious resemblance that Ruth was marrying her father and Heywood his mother, but Ruth was nowhere near her mother-in-law in that relentlessness that the nineteenth century gave its matriarchs as a compensation for their subservience to male rule. Neither was Heywood, despite his modest insistence on his own fecklessness, all that timid. Throughout his life he disarmed and bewildered his mother with charming evasions. He was many times wounded by her salutory put-downs, but in important matters he defied her with a success that his overtly more independent brother and sister came to envy.

Like her Highland Scottish ancestors, Ruth was great at charging a superior foe armed with an eloquence that had the fierce elegance of the bagpipes that sounded the beat of the battle. History sadly tells us what happened to the Highlanders. Behind her gallantry was a self-questioning that she could conceal but not control.

It was not, then, a marriage in which either of them reached for a security never acquired in childhood, and when troubles battered their relationship, it never occurred to them to seek answers in the motto book of their heritage.

After this "something-old, something-new" ceremony, they became not Mr. and Mrs. Heywood Broun but an uneasy alliance that appeared in hotel registers as "Heywood Broun and Ruth Hale, his wife." Marc Connelly told me that this clumsy locution with its last-phrase bow to respectability was suggested by Herbert Bayard Swope, a formidable diplomatist and later Heywood's editor at the New York *World*. Ruth was grumpy about still another compromise and cheerfully cursed Swope for suggesting it.

You could well ask why they didn't just live together and, through the informality of the arrangement, avoid the problems that go with licenses and certificates. In fact the odd title, "Heywood Broun and Ruth Hale, his wife," exactly catches their place in the chart of social history. Vigorous and articulate rebels against the rigidities of their times—social ones in Ruth's case, political ones in Heywood's—they conducted their battles by the rules they didn't believe in, the rules of the enemy, the rules woven right through them when they were children.

In later years they were dutifully to have the extramarital affairs that the twenties demanded as proof of emancipation, but the point of such affairs was supposed to be their casualness. People who actually lived together were still supposed to get married.

The odd wedding didn't work very well and neither did the odd marriage. It was a rickety structure and rancor grew out of that very ricketyness. They weren't happy but they were devoted. They tried to live apart as much as possible and needed each other very much. They disagreed about a great many important things and supported each other's beliefs.

They probably shouldn't have gotten married; they probably should never have had a child; and they probably shouldn't, after seventeen years of marriage, have gotten divorced.

To a small son, convinced that they were all-wise as well as all-powerful, much of what they did seemed bewildering beyond hope of explanation, and to the small son grown older and setting down the story of the three of us, explanations don't come any easier. It's just that the eventual and sad discovery that they were not all-wise makes it easier to under-

stand the story that I am now picking out of my memory like
an archaeologist trying to make a symmetric bowl out of a box
of clay fragments.

• •

Memory for me begins with the first exploratory visit to the
house on Eighty-fifth Street, a brownstone, one of a row of
identical townhouses with stone steps leading up to a glass-
paneled front door and a couple of steps going down to a
basement front entrance for the dining and kitchen area.

I was three years old on the sunny morning in 1921 when
the inspection of the house took place, an event made possible
because Heywood had won a thousand dollars in a poker game,
and, through the help of a lawyer friend, Oscar Bernstein, was
going, if he liked the house, to use this sum as a lever to get
himself under a pyramid of mortgages.

Only now does it occur to me that his urge to buy a house
when he really didn't have enough money to manage it comfortably had to do with a disaster that had long ago struck his
father. Unsuccessful speculation had cost the elder Broun the
house that was the buttress of his nineteenth-century "Look-
what-I-own" self-esteem and sent him off to the social demo-
tion of an apartment. Over and over I was to hear how my
grandmother and her spinster cousin had given the unhappy
man a good breakfast in an undisturbed house, sent him off to
work, and then, with barrels of china and big drays full of
furniture packed at express speed, had raced uptown in time
to give him a good dinner in an apartment where no wisp of
excelsior betrayed the recent arrival.

Perhaps the shy, fat son of that elegant old man was silently
shouting something triumphant to his mother and Cousin
Helen as he opened the door of the handsome place to which
he, still in his early thirties, could come, from an apartment,
with drays and barrels. Wonderfully, too, the house was only

a few blocks from the one his father had lost, and was built in the same style.

As to my thoughts on the occasion, the first was a simple pleasure in the brightness of the front room, a place so sunlit that one could see dancing dust motes in the beams that came through the big front triple window. I was delighted then by the green-tile fireplace with its eerily perfect gas log.

In this first, sharp, organized picture in my collection I see, beyond the fireplace, the electric player piano on the left and the heavily carved kidney-shaped desk on the right. Here, of course, I stop myself and realize that nothing was in the house. It wasn't ours yet, and in any case the desk was to be installed on the floor above.

Psychoanalysts tell us that the distortions of our recollections are instructive. Fantasy has taken me back to that house many times but I can never see it empty. I have no vision of barrels, moving van, or stripped rooms on the day we left it a decade later, and my own self-analytical and therefore suspect guess is that since I came to it from the chaos of nothingness and left it for the chaos of constant dislocation, I don't want anything in it disturbed.

333 West Eighty-fifth Street—there is a cabalistic field day in three people clinging together at a house whose address has three threes—provided, if not stability, at least a kind of shape for Ruth and Heywood and me. The shape was a strange one, a states rights kind of business, with Heywood's independent domain on the first floor, Ruth's on the second, and mine, with the limited rights of a territorial government, on top.

From the basement Mattie Wilson and her husband Earl reached up to us with common sense, efficiency, service that deserves some more exalted name, and understanding of a situation that was not entirely clear to the protagonists themselves.

Visiting between the floors was allowed, but it was always

made clear that the visitor should, upon getting the appropriate sign, take leave; and even I, about to be asked about some piece of misbehavior, always got a "Can I," or, more terrifying, "Can we come in?" We all politely maintained the fiction that I could say no.

Like a great many turn-of-the-century townhouses, ours depended for flexibility on rolling doors, big, heavy brass-wheeled slabs that, pulled back, opened a whole floor for a party.

Heywood's doors were always pulled back, partly because he was, in the clinical sense, a claustrophobe, and partly because in his anxious but unsuccessful battle against overweight, he liked to run the full circle of the first floor while the electric piano urged him on to additional laps with "The Ride of the Valkyrie" and other heavily rhythmic selections from Wagner. I am probably one of the few people who hearing the galloping chords of the "Ride" does not see winged horses rising into the sky, but a heavy-footed man plodding his round on a Persian carpet, perspiring away the pounds that so sadly and quickly he would reacquire.

In the back of his area, comfortingly close to the window that looked out on a barren but open backyard, was the big bed where he piled his mail in wicker laundry baskets that were kept there for what seemed to him a reasonable time, and then emptied to be ready for more unopened and therefore unanswered letters. After a while this caused so much confusion that a series of secretaries, among them another novelist Mildred Gilman, and future Manhattan Borough President Earl Brown, emptied the baskets in an organized way.

Next to the bed was a table and a typewriter where I occasionally saw the strange spectacle of the transformation of Heywood Broun. He would rise from the messy bed with its piles of open books, flattened out at various stages of completion, its baskets of letters, overflowing ashtrays, and crumpled

covers, and sitting at the typewriter he would, with the marvelous, soaring economy of some great dancing master in a
familiar routine, fly across the keys for fifteen or twenty minutes. He would then begin, perhaps as a kind of mantra, or
perhaps as a living metronome, to murmur the name of his
column, "It seems to me, it seems to me, it seems to me," and
keep this up while he read through what he had written, making an occasional correction with a heavy, smudgy copy pencil.
This done, he sent the model piece of personal essay art to his
office and sank back into sloppiness, indecision, and the contemplation of all the problems outside of the easy job of journalism.

• •

Because he was better at doing a job than at getting or
keeping one, Heywood didn't make *The Crimson* at Harvard—
an irony much commented on after he became famous—but
then he failed in almost every goal in college including the
basic matter of getting a degree.

In his freshman year he suffered the twin handicaps of im-
maturity and the fact that the family had universally decided
that he would outstrip his brother Irving, already a sophomore
at Harvard. Whatever Irving accomplished, he was at once told
that Heywood would do it better, and under this pressure
Irving thrived and succeeded while Heywood flunked French
and ethics.

To hide his hurt, Heywood created a number of routines
about his college troubles including the explanation that his
devotion to socialism was due to the fact that he attended all
the economics lectures about the validity of Marxism, but cut
all the spring classes in which its fallacies were exposed, because he went to Fenway Park to see Tris Speaker, Harry
Hooper, and Duffy Lewis, the classic Red Sox outfield crew.

He also said that he endeavored to speak freshman French

in Paris and found that it was spoken only at Harvard.

Freshmen suffered hazards at Harvard far beyond learning lists of French irregular verbs, however. Attendance was compulsory for these innocents at a hygiene course known as "Smut One." Here they were shown tinted lantern slides depicting the horrid results of venereal infection. Going against faculty logic, as freshmen often did, Heywood became convinced that if sexual adventure flourished despite the spectacular and lethal decay that it caused, it must be more marvelous than any poet had cracked it up to be. Within a week he had been picked up by a prostitute in Scollay Square and shortly thereafter he experienced the result of Harvard's cautionary lecture, a case of gonorrhea. The humiliation of having to report it and undergo treatment left such a scar that when, years later, he was shown his infant son with eyes blackened by silver nitrate, a routine precaution against the disease, he almost blurted out, "Oh my God, who told you!"

It remained a wonder to me that after what seemed to be a steady series of mishaps at Harvard, from athletic injury through social disease to academic failure, he was always braving snowstorms to root and freeze at the Yale game.

He seemed ungraduated in the truest sense of the word.

The lost credits were never made up and the wound never healed. He used to ask if anybody had ever been given an honorary bachelor's degree. He said he would take no comfort from some meaningless Doctorate of Humane Letters, the kind of thing handed out to celebrities and wealthy alumni. He hoped that Harvard might recognize his contributions to journalism with the simplest, lowest, and to him most desired of its academic distinctions.

When President Lowell of Harvard served on the Commission that validated the decision in the Sacco and Vanzetti case, Heywood wrote a column that included the line, "Shall Harvard now be known as Hangman's House?" Heywood's intransigence in the matter of Sacco and Vanzetti was to cost him his job on the *World*, but worse than that, he felt, was the fact that it ended hope for the honorary B.A. Because he was big, Heywood had been a successful athlete at Horace Mann School, but this easy road to college status was closed when he wrecked his knee in a freshman basketball game. At six foot four inches (characteristically, he always announced his height as "six-three and three-quarters," and tried by stooping to bring himself down a couple of inches below that), he was big enough to play on any 1907 basketball team, but the clumsiness born of his shyness led him to trip over a stray piece of equipment in the Yale gym and limp out of the athletic arena.

He had a single literary triumph, getting a story published in a college magazine, *The Advocate*. Called "Red Magic," it was a sentimental and flowery legend of the urgent power of young love. Later he rewrote it and used it in his column, but in the newspaper version he enclosed the narrative in the whimsical irony that had become the eggshell armor of his vulnerability.

His other Harvard triumph appears to have been as a poker player. Playing for somewhat smaller stakes than those that would heap the table at the Algonquin Thanatopsis Club, he announced triumphantly on the flyleaf of a play called *The London Merchant*, assigned for Professor Baker's English 56, that the fifty-five cents needed to buy it had been won over a two-month period of poker from his friend Osmond Fraenkel.

Baker and Charles Copeland, great men in their day, were his English teachers at Harvard and were it not for the misfortune of his nongraduation, I suspect he might have followed them into the clubby gentility of the academic world. Equally, with the smallest of nudges Heywood could have become a successful whimsical novelist of the second rank, turning out things in imitation of his literary idols, Leonard Merrick and William J. Locke. The heroes of Heywood's favorites among the works of these now-forgotten writers were charming, passive men who were chivied into sedentary romantic situations by masterful women and felicitous circumstance.

I remember Heywood urging on me Locke's *The Morals of Marcus Ordeyne,* and my finding it to be pretty milk and water stuff. The story of a shy, scholarly man fought over by two beautiful women seemed to me to be the sort of thing where you skipped ahead to see who won and then forgot the whole business. I was twelve years old when the book was given to me, and the rattle of teacups did not seem a satisfactory substitute for the boom of the *Hispaniola*'s guns in *Treasure Island.* Why did he give me such a book at such a time? Why did he give Merrick's *Conrad in Quest of His Youth* to someone who was not even a youth? Silly perhaps, but I thank him for sparing me *Hans Brinker* and *The Wind in the Willows.*

The genteel literary direction of Heywood's life was diverted abruptly, however, when his father announced that four years was *it* for higher education and that he had, through a friend who owned racehorses, gotten Heywood a job on *The Morning Telegraph.* It was a paper that divided its attention between the stage and the turf, and accounts of war and natural disaster popped up only in terms of how they might interrupt race meetings or postpone Broadway options. The paper was sometimes called "The chorus girl's breakfast."

Grandfather, who liked to hide his selfishness in clouds of club-land euphemism, referred to this abandonment of his son's education as an adventure in belles lettres, a proper sort of career for a gentleman's younger son if he weren't interested in Holy Orders. Anyone less suited to the reporter's life than shy, sensitive Heywood Broun could hardly be imagined— except that, of course, he made a huge success of it.

One of the reasons for his success was the fact that the typewriter was to him what the mask of someone else's identity is to the actor. From his place behind the machine he spoke easily and well. All shyness fell away and, as his fingers rattled

• WHOSE LITTLE BOY ARE YOU? •

over the letters, there emerged a personality never at a loss for words or opinions. Psychoanalysts call those activities that, successfully pursued, earn us the money to pay for our hours of self-examination, "conflict-free areas." Heywood at the typewriter was out of reach of the phobias that, like a ring of wolves, surrounded the campfire of his keyboard.

His toughness as a writer was not something that developed when the genial essayist of the twenties became the political crusader of the thirties.

As soon as he was allowed a printed opinion he was demonstrating that he didn't care who got mad at his written words, and later as a theater critic he was as punishing as the most curmudgeonly of his colleagues.

Sued by an actor for an exceptionally savage review, he won the suit but then branded the man's next performance as "Not up to his usual standard."

He, along with Alexander Woollcott for a time, was barred from the Shubert theatres on account of sour notices. He and Woollcott were also to have been the targets of an onstage outcry from John Barrymore, who was upset over their opinions of a play called *The Butterfly* by his wife, Michael Strange.

"I'm going out in front of the curtain tonight and I will denounce those vultures Broun and Woollcott. It will make headlines in all the papers," he told a family conference.

"No, there will be a much bigger headline," snarled the most imitated voice of its time—"Lionel Barrymore strangles brother in dressing room before performance."

At his critical debut, Ethel was supposed to have said frostily that she didn't care to have her work assessed by a baseball writer.

This was, of course, nonsense born of irritability. Ethel Barrymore, a fanatic Giants fan, would probably have esteemed John McGraw's good opinion over that of Bernard Shaw; and the fact that Heywood was a friend of Christy Mathewson was reason enough for the friendship that soon sprang up between him and all the Barrymores.

In the course of her press work for Arthur Hopkins, Ruth saw a good deal of John and perhaps it was because of her relationship with a critic that Barrymore, seeing her dozing in the auditorium during rehearsal, rushed backstage to make up his hands with a set of warts, carbuncles, and claws so that, standing behind her, he could wake her by touching her face with them. On that occasion Ruth was supposed to have used words even Barrymore had never heard.

• •

In direct speech Ruth used language with assurance and grace, but writing for her was painful and slow. The reasons why Ruth became a writer were certainly not part of the autobiography she gave me. This narrative was precise, extensive, and, I realized much later, heavily edited.

She never, for instance, told me anything about her aspirations as an artist or her art school days in Philadelphia. This academy must have been her first step on the great escape from home and should have been the source of a large number of memories made vivid by the excitement and nervousness that surrounded the move. If I had not been an egotistic and incurious little boy, I guess I would have asked, but as it was, I accepted her accomplished portrait sculptures as some sort of hobby. I still have a little wax bust of myself modeled when I was about five. It is recognizable when compared to photographs taken then, but the pictures show a wary expression missing from the little three-dimensional me.

A simple desire to defy seemed a good enough reason for her to paint a huge, squatting, red and green fiend figure on her bedroom wall. It thumbed its nose at the world outside her room and she called it a picture of her soul. Many years later it peered startlingly out at me from the pages of a magazine, turning out to be an Aztec devil. Remembering it, I find it a fair soul portrait with its odd grin and the essential harmlessness of the mocking gesture. There is a sort of wistfulness in its fierceness that seems quite clear. I wonder whether she thought so, too.

The official résumé of Ruth Hale as passed on to her son began with the bad years in Rogersville, Tennessee, where it appears that the very idea of feminism had never entered anybody's mind. It was "unladylike" in Rogersville to come as close to masculinity as to sing contralto, and Ruth's fine voice was ruined by being forced upward to the appropriately "feminine" register. Ladies read only genteel literature and she had to get through a certain amount of Sir Walter Scott every day. She did this while leaning on a backboard in aid of a proper posture. Only occasional horseback rides with her father, whom she loved but never made vivid by description, muted the monotony of these terrible times. It was during those rides that she took the first steps in her career of shock, refusing the sidesaddle that her mother, aunts, and neighbors thought appropriate. Her mother, aunts, and neighbors were all part of that group she described as "a basket of snakes" in urging me never to visit her hometown.

I felt guilty many years later when, playing a very small part in a movie in Knoxville, I became a temporary celebrity. I was surrounded by reporters and photographers to the bewilderment of the film's press agent, who kept offering interviews with Robert Preston and Jean Simmons, the stars of the piece. "Oh no," was the xenophobic cry from the press, "we want Mr. Broun because he is a Rogersville boy!"

How pleased the grandmother, aunts, and neighbors would have been! How pleased probably were those unknown relatives still in Rogersville to see their town jostling the Cuban missile crisis on the front page of the Knoxville *Journal.* I had said the right things in the interview about how I regretted that a busy shooting schedule kept me from visiting the ancestral home, but I wondered if Ruth would have wanted me to fire a blast for her. I wonder now if she hated the place as uncomplicatedly as she said. She certainly spent a lot of time flouting its rules, but you can't help but be surprised at how many of them she seemed to have remembered.

One of the new rules that involved me was the ban on calling her "Mother," "Mom," or any of the many varieties between and around. She was to be Ruth and Heywood was to be Heywood. This was supposed to get us all out of the spiderweb tangle that she saw as symbolic of family relationships.

I found this embarrassing and was always having to explain it to outsiders who thought I was being a smart aleck and to schoolmates who thought my parents were crazy and that I should at least call them my mom and dad while I was out of earshot. I was either too loyal or too frightened to do this until well into my teens when, to teachers and other authority figures, I would occasionally refer to "my mother and father."

So far underground were my rebellions that I didn't even know they existed, and for most of the time I defended the freedom that I disliked, the freedom that pretended that, since we were on a first-name basis, we were equals.

Ruth broke out of her familial web at eighteen. As she told it to me, she simply went north and shortly thereafter became, for the Philadelphia *Public Ledger,* the country's first woman movie critic.

The only apparent talisman she had in this sensational rise was a sentence handed her by an aunt, one of those elderly autocrats who wear cameo brooches like medals and warm their withered frames with crocheted shawls whose makings kept their hands busy through long hours of genealogical discussion.

"If you have any trouble up there, Lillie Ruth, you just tell them that you're the niece of Miss Richards of Culpepper County, Virginia, and everything will be all right."

That my mother had once had a name as squashily feminine as Lillie Ruth led to a lot of questions that she brushed off. Maybe that's why I, diverted, never got any answer about how this remarkable rise was accomplished or about the time she spent at Drexel Institute of the Arts.

Long after her death, I found in the flyleaf of one of her books a beautifully detailed little drawing of a row of houses in one of which she may have lived while going to school. Looking at its easy skill (particularly impressive to one who can't draw an oblong without missing a corner), I wondered why during those last idle years she had spent so much time with crosswords and jigsaws.

In any case, Ruth's shift from art to journalism was a good break for her brothers Shelton and Richard. With the money the writing career produced, she pulled them both out of the Rogersville "basket," sent them to college, and out into a wider world than the one extending from the courthouse cannon to the edge of grandfather's farm.

Her brothers launched, Ruth decided on a wider world for herself and moved to New York where she was drama critic for *Vogue,* a theatrical press agent, and a reporter for *The New York Times.* While there, she told me, she wrote the first set of accounts of the Hundred Neediest Cases, the paper's annual charity. It appears that the organized groups that had been solicited failed to come up with enough stories. She then filled out the hundred with cases she had observed in covering family court, an audacious and, as the *Times* put it, irresponsible thing to do. There was a lot of trouble about digging up and helping the people who, upon leaving the court, had disappeared back into the depths of misery.

As to the courtship of Ruth Hale and Heywood Broun, there was given to me only a single anecdote, a cute set piece that does nothing to explain the barbed-steel tether of dependence that held them together even after their painful and pointless divorce.

"We were sitting on a bench in Central Park," is the way Ruth tells it, "when a squirrel came along and perched in front of us, chattering and begging. 'He wants a peanut,' I said. 'Why don't you go and get some?' Sitting there, big and lazy in the sunshine, Heywood smiled and said, 'I tell you what. I'll give him a nickel and he can go buy his own.' At that moment I decided he was the kind of person I wanted to marry."

The only thing at all convincing about the story is the picture of Heywood substituting charm for effort. The rest sounds like something made up later to explain something essentially inexplicable. Still, it's the only picture in my scrapbook. My inquiries about who came before this pairing and how it progressed from the payoff of the squirrel to the church never seemed to get much but mumbles, although Heywood had a little lost-love set piece about Lydia Lopokova, the Russian dancer who was later to marry the economist Maynard Keynes. Heywood met Miss Lopokova when she briefly joined the Provincetown Players to add a little acting skill to her dancing, and they were for a few weeks a striking couple—the big man, made even larger by a voluminous and shapeless fur coat, bending adoringly over the vivid, tiny little woman. They must have looked like some Aesopian pairing of a bear and a bird.

The depth of the relationship was suggested by a letter Lady Keynes wrote to one of Heywood's biographers. "Our engagement was so brief and so long ago that I'm afraid I can't remember anything about Heywood at all."

As to Ruth, I heard murmurs from friends of hers about a broken romance in Philadelphia (in art school perhaps?), and one or two of her books have unknown names written in as the givers, but her cupboard of memory, like Heywood's, was never really opened to me. They just both reached in and picked out pieces for display.

• W H O S E L I T T L E B O Y A R E Y O U ? •

• •

However they got there, I pick from my own cupboard the memories of 333 West Eighty-fifth Street, the place where for a short time, Ruth, Heywood, and Woodie found a way of living—together by choice, divided by choice—that satisfied them and mystified everyone. Choosing pictures of the house off my shadow shelves, I can go up the brownstone steps outside, slide across the sill to the front window, and enter through it, a romantic if inconvenient way of getting in—and oddly never used by a burglar. I cross Heywood's front room, stepping around piles of books, and go up the stairs to Ruth's floor, and, swinging on the newel post at the end of the short hall, start, under the watery and patchy illumination shed by the skylight, to climb to my own domain. I wonder now, as I always did, whether the architect had had a stroke about the time he designed my floor, or whether, getting some other job then, he had left the design to be finished by some failed student whose duties were usually limited to sharpening the pencils and keeping the coffee hot.

Where the floors below me were designed with flexibility and grandeur and permitted an easy progression from sizable salon to appropriately privacy-tight compartments, my floor was fudged together very oddly. My bedroom, at the front of the house, was flanked by the large open stairwell that had hanging over it a tiny maid's room that was occupied in our case by occasional live-in baby-sitters. If this was a servant's floor, however, it would be hard to explain why my room opened through an elegant archway into a large dressing room complete with bathtub and basin but, disastrously, no toilet. This necessity was all the way at the other end of the hall, and to a small boy anxious to be perfect, but not yet ready to achieve such a high degree of accomplishment, this meant occasional shame and terror as I failed to cover the necessary distance in time.

I pretty well abandoned the use of the dressing room after a large patch of the ceiling fell into the tub with a kettledrum boom. I wasn't in it at the time, or the boom would have been muffled, but the sound, which bounced me out of bed like a near miss in the Blitz, convinced me that hazards lay all around me, and that area became a kind of Badlands outside the cozy confines of the bedroom. Even this was not completely safe, however, and there was noise that nearly matched the crash of the falling ceiling when my bed, once supposed to have held the Marquis de Lafayette, collapsed under my inconsiderable weight. The dressing room ceiling was never, as I remember, patched up but the bed was pulled to its feet and nested in a webbing of rope that held it firm for its next task. Having held a Revolutionary hero, it now seemed ready to be my deathbed.

I was four years old when a doctor looked down at the little blue creature retching feebly in the middle of the bed and announced, "This child is dying." Under the circumstances it wasn't a bad guess, but it would have been more tactful to make the statement out in the hall. Ruth obviously thought so for she said, I was told, "Don't you think he speaks English, you dumb son of a bitch? Pack your bag and get out!" Later I used to see that doctor at my grandmother's house. He looked like a character actor's idea of a physician, complete with spats and a little pointed beard. He never apologized and I never gloated, partly because for years after he was bundled down the stairs I thought he was going to be right pretty soon.

With the prediction still chilling her heart, Ruth set out to restore me through the oldest of therapies, a mixture of rocking, warming against the heart, and the wordless murmur of encouraging sounds. Because I want so much to remember this moment of closeness I have constructed a picture of the whole business. In the picture I see the room as very dark; I see the doctor snapping shut his little useless bag and then I give myself to the peace of exhaustion mixed with security.

Like my recollection of the first view of the house, this picture is rich with detail that is as well organized as it is unlikely, and I am sure that the whole thing was a lot messier than what I have permitted myself to remember.

In a rather chilling moment of prophecy, Heywood had visited a near fatal case of croup on Pat, the "Boy" of his novel *The Boy Grew Older*, written a year before my sickness, although in the book it is the father who holds the child close through the crisis. When, many years later, I sang on the stage of Philharmonic Hall in a benefit performance of Marc Blitzstein's *The Cradle Will Rock*, it occurred to me, amid my fears as to why I had let myself in for this, that Pat had left the newspaper business and his father to become a serious singer. How consciously was life imitating art?

Nobody ever figured out what caused the forty-eight hours of internal tumult during which I emptied myself of everything but life itself. The name given me for the specific ailment was acidosis, a name that is not used anymore. Looking it up, I discovered that the dregs remaining after much of yourself has been poured away consist largely of acids and that it isn't good to be so largely acidulous. That night, and the days following—the days in which Ruth pulled me back to life—make me think suddenly of the remark of an old Navajo that hospital doctors were worthless because they stuck a piece of glass in your mouth to find out something you already knew—that you had a fever—and then went away and left you. How superior, he said, was the medicine man who gave you his full attention through eight hours of dancing and chanting. The days in which Ruth gave me her full attention got me back on an even keel, but I was much lower in the water than I had been. The jolly chubby child of the early photographs, the laughing lump of healthy pink fat, had become a rail-thin wisp with the anxious, self-concerned expression of the professional invalid.

I was to continue in this almost to the end of my teens and

I adjusted my hopes and expectations to the feeling, very strong and destined to grow stronger, that I was a disappointment and a nuisance, and that my troubles were due to poisons generated within me by a vague general badness that was my own fault. Aside from all this hysteria there was the objective fact, admitted by all, that I had substantially ceased to grow and seemed to drop further and further behind my age group.

It was, then, as a kind of charmless Tiny Tim that I suffered through the overpowering holiday gatherings at Grandmother and Grandfather Broun's.

On these occasions the dark old-fashioned dining room at the inner end of a railroad flat, crammed with all the mahogany from the town house, steamed with good food and good humor. Although after a few years I began to realize that many of the jokes, ritually told each year in almost exactly the same words, had an edge of ancient malice.

Some years Heywood told the one about meeting Grandfather on the street and some years it was left to Uncle Irving, but there was always a good deal of merriment when we arrived at the punch line, "You're nice-looking boys. Do you live on this block?" Grandfather was supposed to have said this to his sons after a return from one of his multimonth stays at his club.

Grandmother would then smile and say that the reason she opposed divorce was that the first twenty-five years of her marriage having been made miserable by her husband's departure from the house every time she tried to argue with him—"If you need me, Etta, I'll be at the club"—this had been followed with twenty-odd years of happiness, years made happy apparently by the simple device of giving him his way in everything. That she gave him his way in anything amazed the rest of us, because my grandmother was formidable in the elegantly imperious manner of a Henry James character whose hotel reservation has been lost.

• WHOSE LITTLE BOY ARE YOU? •

Cousin Helen always got to tell the story about Grandmother and the street car. Waiting on the wrong corner, Mrs. Broun had raised her umbrella several times to no avail, ignoring the pointing fingers of the motorman who tried to show her where she should wait. Eventually a policeman, routinely stopping traffic at that corner, presented her with an immobile trolley, and she irritably tapped on its glass door. The motorman went through his pointing, and Grandmother went through the glass with the handle of her umbrella. The policeman started toward her, the driver opened the remains of the door to protest, and each was given a special look that had the effect of a paralyzing ray. It was compounded of such simple things as arched eyebrows and a raised chin, but to describe it that way is like saying that a lightning bolt is a flash and a pop. She deposited her nickel and went downtown.

Years later Grandmother wrote to her landlord saying that if the heat didn't improve, she would write to President Truman. Amused at this, the landlord, an acquaintance of Irving's, called him and read him the letter. There was a pause and then in a voice become once again boyishly uncertain, Irving said, "Gee, you better fix the furnace or she will write to the president and he'll have you punished."

At the dinners Irving got to tell the story about Heywood, big for his age, still in long curls at twelve, being called "Lilacs" by the boys on the block. Angry, but not angry enough to fight, Heywood would summon Irving to be his champion and black eyes would be exchanged, for which Irving was often punished. Eventually both boys persuaded their father, briefly home from the club, to sneak Heywood to a barber shop. Shown the result, Grandmother was stricken, and rushed to the shop to gather souvenir locks. I suspect Grandfather went back to the club, perhaps returning in time to save Irving from the police after he threw snowballs at the Crown Prince of Germany. The occasion being well in advance of World War

I, the assault had nothing to do with patriotism. It seems simply to have been the concatenation of easily moldable snow and a silly-looking man in a silly-looking uniform going slowly by in an open car. The police called Grandmother, who sent Grandfather with the dual instruction that he was to free his son and see to it that his name was expunged from the record.

God knows what blandishments and bribes my grandfather distributed, possibly some champagne from the vaults of his wine business. But he showed up with Irving to be met not with congratulations but with the question, "Is his name still on the blotter?" What curious honesty compelled him to tell the unacceptable truth I never found out, but he was made to regret it, and going back out the door played a few games of billiards, at which he was a champion, before returning to announce that our name was cleansed.

Although carving in those days was as much a gentleman's accomplishment as billiards, Grandfather, perhaps not wishing to bring a blade near his valuable game player's hands, left this task to Cousin Helen, and there was a whole series of ritual jokes about the thinness of her turkey slices.

Heywood and Irving, working with the easy give and take of old vaudeville comics, would affect to make Cousin Helen's precisely cut portions float away because of their gossamer quality and a big laugh-getter was reading the newspaper through a suspended piece of meat, Irving putting on his glasses to spell out some previously learned line.

Cousin Helen, who was as steely as Grandmother but jollier about it, had taught Heywood, Irving, and Aunt Virginia at Horace Mann School and still regarded them as liable to be sent out into the hall if things went too far. In the relaxed atmosphere of the holiday, however, she would smile, say that even without her glasses she could see two great boobies, and then with a deft stroke of her tools would cut the neck and a piece of the back for Uncle Fritz.

· W H O S E L I T T L E B O Y A R E Y O U ? ·

Uncle Fritz, Grandmother's brother, was a great favorite with the children but not, apparently, with anyone else. When not at the table, he sat in an alcove off the living room smoking cheap cigars and telling adventure stories about life around the copper mines of South America to my cousins and me.

Although I did not know it at the time, Uncle Fritz was required to come to midday dinner every Sunday to collect his allowance from Grandfather. He was not allowed to bring the mistress with whom he eventually celebrated a fiftieth anniversary, presumably on a weekday, and he was not allowed to marry her—she being socially unacceptable—on pain of losing the allowance.

There is a good deal of nostalgia now for those grand old extended family dinners, and couples trying to make holiday fun over a couple of game hens often sigh for three generations of merrymakers pulling old chestnuts and new wishbones.

Looking at the bunch around our table, however, and rating the fun at one to ten, there seemed to me a number of ones and twos. Uncle Wyman Herbert, Aunt Virginia's handsome, silent husband, quit coming early in the game, and his silence grew to the point that he didn't speak to her for five years. Aunt Vera, Irving's wife, always showed up but always looked as if she were sorry. She felt that everybody disapproved of her, and this was substantially true. Aunt Vera drank, possibly because of the disapproval, and nobody brought up the question of the chicken and the egg. The only person who went out of her way to be nice to Vera was Ruth, who didn't much approve of most of the Brouns.

Rated by me at ten were my three big, handsome cousins. They seemed to me to be happy as only big, handsome people could be, and their full hearty laughs at Heywood's and Irving's jokes rattled on me like raps from a hammer. Drummond Herbert was as handsome as his father and a good deal merrier, and Kathryn Herbert had dimples. Irving's daughter Almeda had a sans souci chuckle and was beautiful. One summer, and one summer only, the whole family from eldest to youngest spent at Atlantic Highlands, New Jersey. I think the only person who had a good time that year was Uncle Fritz, who got to stay in the city and get his allowance by mail. The camaraderie that we could manage through the length of a holiday afternoon and evening was rubbed off by the strain of extended pretended good nature. When I tried to kill Kathryn with a canoe paddle, I was not any nervier than anyone else, just easier to goad because of my painful and constant sense of inferiority. Only my weakness and the lightness of the paddle saved Kathryn from serious damage. Even the fact that I alone in the family was able to identify at great distances the yachts involved in that summer's America's Cup races did nothing to increase my self-esteem.

Some of my distinctions, indeed, made me feel worse. I know that at Christmas and birthdays Grandfather would give me presents much superior to the gifts handed out to the cousins, but I knew this wasn't because he liked me better but because I was the crown prince, Heywood III, the only boy Broun—and wasn't that a terrible pity.

Once, looking down at his plate of bony offal, Uncle Fritz had been bold enough to ask for some meatier part of the holiday bird, and had been met with the icy adjuration, "Eat what is set before you, Fritz!"

Pushing my succulent slices of breast around the plate at that moment, I remember a rare spasm of concern for somebody other than myself, a feeling that when one gets to be seventy years old like Fritz this sort of treatment was awful and wrong. Right after that, though, was the thought that Uncle Fritz, turkey-neck diet and all, had won the love of someone who had held to it unwaveringly for half a century. Like someone whose move in the Uncle Wiggly game had taken him into the maw of the Skillery-Skallory Alligator, I lost two turns and went back to the bottom. I think I would have cried right there in the middle of all the holiday hope, but somebody would have asked why, and I didn't have any story to cover this and would have to mention Uncle Fritz, who didn't need any more attention than he was getting. I suppose another shot at the blameless Kathryn might have relieved my feelings, but that would have become one of the oft-repeated stories for the future and I didn't think much of that.

I think what I did was ask Cousin Helen to tell the story of the hairdresser who almost succeeded in hypnotizing Grandmother and her when they were in Switzerland. While Cousin Helen, with glittering eyes, speculated on the vile motives of the hairdresser and how deep their drowsiness had become before some fortunate accident saved them, I gloomed over the plate Uncle Fritz would have been glad to get at.

I don't remember when Uncle Fritz died. I imagine he did it as quietly as possible so that a graceful arrangement might be made to continue the allowance to his non-widow; but whenever it was, he had a long run of it, extending nearly to eighty. Years later at Irving's funeral, I noticed that Uncle Fritz' stone in the family plot in Brooklyn lay askew on the ground. At first I thought maybe nobody had ever bothered to set it up, and then it occurred to me that perhaps he had reached up and pulled it over so that he could continue in that present but inconspicuous state that seemed best to suit his needs.

Of course, with a little shift of emphasis the Brouns became as suffocatingly jolly as any of those colorful families that parade their eccentricities through the best-seller lists.

Generations remember Clarence Day's father as the most lovable curmudgeon of stage and screen, but Ruth, who spent a lot of time visiting with the younger Day as he crouched in the wheelchair to which arthritis early confined him, told me that Clarence hated life with his father and wrote the cheery books as an effort to reduce the pressures of his passionate resentment.

Perhaps dour little Woodie is, in his puny spite, not fair to the hearty healthies who towered around him at Grandmother's table.

Certainly a very different picture of it is drawn in a letter I got after Heywood's death from a lady named Frank Royers Brooks, who, at the age of twelve, had gone home with Virginia from Horace Mann School and found a warmth that still rises—a comforting sound of long-ago laughter—from the yellowed pages of her letter.

At the brownstone high stoop house, 140 West 87th Street, where every afternoon after school hours we all gathered for tea, and where on Sunday afternoons the size of the crowd of young people suggested a reception, Mrs. Broun presided. She was always at home in the afternoon. She made us welcome, was interested in our lives, our interests and our hopes. She was tolerant and undemanding, always kind and sympathetic. An intellectual herself, she was rarely gifted in mind and heart and put everyone at his ease.

Grandfather is more recognizable to me in the Brooks portrait as "He flitted in and out of 140 from his clubs and his golf, shooting and his outstanding bridge. I think his overrun house bewildered him when he found us, as he usually did, in possession of his home."

When it came to Christmas apparently houses for blocks around were stripped of adolescent children as they hurried to the gaiety available at the Brouns'.

"I can't count the years," wrote Mrs. Brooks, "we gathered at the Brouns' on Xmas night. There was always the tree, jokes and poems to be read and gifts exchanged, supper and dancing and gladness and Xmas spirit."

There comes over me a mournful feeling that I was so busy

looking at my boils and carbuncles, real and spiritual, that I missed out on a lot of foaming, sparkling happiness. Then I wish I could ask Uncle Fritz how it all looked from the corner where he waited for his envelope.

Frank Brooks wrote that "To the boys and girls who had no strong home ties, Mrs. Broun gave them a feeling that 'they belonged' and with the rest of us, she adopted our families with us and gave us two homes."

That would probably have given Uncle Fritz a discreet chuckle quickly covered with a cloud from his deplorable cigar, but it wasn't any less true. It seems more a question of where you sit.

•   •

Frank Brooks first came to the Broun house when she was twelve. When I started going to the Broun apartment my chances of reaching the age of twelve did not look very good, a prospect that distorted my views on everything.

The doctor had proved wrong on the occasion he pronounced me dying, but I just thought he was a few months or years off. Fearful with every subsequent fever that the time was now arriving, I constantly calculated life spans and measured the success of every existence by its length. To this day when reading of some historical character in a reference book, my first act is to look up the years of beginning and ending in order to do the arithmetic. No matter how full or happy the reported life, I don't count it a success until it reaches the Biblical allowance of three score years and ten. By my standards, Uncle Fritz was a winner and Alexander the Great a loser.

I suppose I must have talked about this worry and there wasn't any way completely to dispel it, since I think Ruth and Heywood were not much more hopeful than I was, but Ruth came up with a thought one evening in my sixth or seventh year that shaped the nature of the first and for a time strongest of my ambitions—survival. We were going through a book of photographs together and came across a portrait head of an Indian chief. I remarked admiringly on his great age, made obvious by the web of lines that lay across his strong, eroded, leathery face. I said I hoped that I could live long enough to wear that look, and Ruth said something that I can still hear, echoing at the back of memory.

"When you get that old," she said, "you don't mind dying." She went on to explain that a time would come when what you mostly felt was tired, when all your friends had already died, your children had grown up, and you had accomplished everything you wanted, or had discovered that you were never going to accomplish it. At this point sleep would seem tremendously welcome, even the last one from which there is no waking.

Of course, for me, this age of satiation and exhaustion lay far ahead, but with luck and caution perhaps I could reach it. In any case, there was tremendous excitement in the notion that, like some scientifically provable state of blessedness, there was a time and place where I need not be afraid, a state where I wouldn't mind hearing the phrase "He's dying."

I wonder sometimes whether she understood the old Indian's feeling so fully because she was already, with her friends alive, her child ungrown, and her ambitions unrealized, beginning to feel a premonitory weariness about the state of her life.

In any case, she kept the dark share of her thoughts to herself and gave me the immensely comforting notion that my convulsive grip on life might loosen at my own wish, and that letting go might at last be my idea. In the meantime, I went back to hanging on as tightly and fearfully as Harold Lloyd hanging from the clock hand high above the street in *Safety Last*.

I wonder too how different my life might have been if ambition had been reined in right there and I had never had to give subsequent thought to anything but the cautiously triumphant passage of the days and years.

I thought very hard about this when, in the midst of my pointlessly painful bout of middle-aged depression, I had occasion as a CBS news correspondent to interview an old black horse trainer at the Charlestown racetrack in West Virginia. John Wright was much admired throughout the racing world, not because of his success, which had been limited, but for the bright liveliness of his spirit and the jovial gallantry with which he faced the uncertainties of life in the back barns of secondary tracks.

When I met him he had two horses, two teeth, and about twenty-seven big safety pins fastened to the legs of his pants, pins with which he could fasten the complicated bandages that supported the wounded old legs of his color-bearers. As we sat down to talk, surrounded by the daunting apparatus of the electronic interview, his face radiated confidence and goodwill. His smile had none of the furtive bonhomie of those grins that hope to catch crumbs by currying favor. In its clear directness it would have graced the face of the trainer of a Derby favorite, instead of the seamed but serene countenance of a man who might today be able to pay part of a hay bill with a fourth-place finish in a race for nonwinners.

The face of the interviewer, stretching painfully into a professional welcome, was made small by a combination of the misery that went with him everywhere and a fresh shame that he should be so droopy while the parlously placed old man waiting for his questions so obviously had his sunny side up, a rainbow round his shoulder, and a certainty that God being in his heaven, all was right with the world.

He told me that his crippled crocks were showing pleasing signs of recovering their old speed and that he had every hope that a couple of purses would permit him to upgrade his stable and get back to the major tracks where he had operated in the twenties and thirties.

Depressed people take a grim pleasure in ticking over the superiorities of other persons, and by the time I finished talking to John Wright I had added him up and found that he ought to be some sort of lesson to me, except that I seemed unable in my dark mood to accept any instruction much beyond when to start talking on camera and when to stop.

Shortly after the interview, I was talking to a wise friend and asking him, since he was wise, why the old man had the world by the tail while I, like some inept child at a birthday party, had dropped the tail, didn't have any idea where the donkey was, and was crying into my blindfold and wishing I hadn't been invited to play the pin-the-tail game.

"That's not hard to understand," said the friend. "You tell me that when Wright was ten years old he was loaded into a truck in Arkansas to help take some horses to a railhead. Somehow he got shut into the boxcar with the horses and roared off to Chicago, a frightened, bewildered little boy who was never to see his parents again and who had every prospect of being stomped to death by big frightened animals. At the moment that his full situation in all its hopelessness came home to him, he formed his life's ambition to stay alive. He has fully realized it with, in the Biblical sense, two years on top of his three score and ten. He has done it with honor and good humor and is a success.

"You, Woodie, are Heywood Broun's boy, Ruth Hale's boy. It's not enough for you to survive. You have to be a gentleman. You must fill big pairs of shoes, follow in footsteps, must not give way to anger because you have been given so much more than others that you are not entitled to anger, must live up to your heritage, must be grateful for it, and most of all must not be allowed unhappiness because unhappiness would reflect unfavorably on those wonderful people Ruth and Heywood. Of course, you're a failure. What else could you be?"

I can't say that I burst into a big smile and thanked him, but I have often since wished that I had stayed with the idea that ripeness is all and that getting to tomorrow without trampling on loved ones is the aim and end of life.

Meanwhile, back at the sickroom, doctors more tactful but not more cheerful came frequently as unexplained coughs, fevers, and bouts of boils indicated that acids, or something produced by acids, were still gnawing away at my well-being.

My third-floor kingdom seemed narrowed to the confines of my bed, and the flashing silver of thermometer tips waving through the air was the baton that set my pace.

One of the doctors I remember with pleasure because whatever boil lance or bottle of tonic he removed from his bag, he also removed a small movie projector. Setting this up while I pursed the thermometer, he would, right after reading the glass column, pull down the shades and distract me from my drear, repetitive problems by showing on the wall of my room the endlessly diverting problems of Charlie Chase or Harry Langdon, running up and down the wonderful wide streets of long-ago Los Angeles ahead of runaway cars and silently shouting people. No more than the other doctors did he seem to have any definitive answers, but he, for brief stretches, kept me from worrying about a principal concern of this time—Were they going to send me away again as they had after the big near-death battle with the acidosis?

As I remember vividly my arrival at the house on Eighty-fifth Street, so I remember with equal clarity the first extended departure from it. I got the news of the prospective exile while I was standing by a bookcase in Heywood's room. The second shelf was exactly at the level of my head and I tried to distract myself by spelling out titles—I was an early reader—to keep from taking in his news, which was that I was going to California to get well. Heywood, sitting on a bed to achieve a more intimate level and not give me the crusher from way up there, told me that Elsie MacKnight, a jolly, friendly trained nurse whom I already knew, was going to take me there and that I certainly would have a very good time.

I was uncertain of this because I didn't know where or what California was, but I knew it wasn't Eighty-fifth Street, and I wanted to stay in my room in my house more than I had ever wanted anything in a life that although short was already full of wishes.

I said in some simple confused way that I had been encouraged to make decisions and one that I wanted to make was about not going to California but, of course, I went.

I supposed naturally enough that I was not being sent away to get healthy—What was healthy about this California?—but that I was being put out of sight because I was an unattractive nuisance, something to be set outside of the house to be taken away.

Elsie MacKnight had friends in Los Angeles, and I remember a birthday party at their house with presents and a cake and even some friendly kids dug up with God knows what patient effort.

None of this kindness kept me from behaving badly to Elsie, who was the only member of the junta I could get at. I still remember the intensity of pleasure mixed with fear when she opened a traveling bag into which I had squeezed a tube of glue. I see with terrible joy the sticky stocking adhering to her hand and, dangling from the end of the stocking, a white ivory shoehorn.

No Hollywood treats seemed able to weaken my fixed feeling that happiness would only lie between West End Avenue and Riverside Drive in Upper Manhattan. I was given the pleasure of a day with the reigning child star, Jackie Coogan. Temporarily grounded while a cap was being made for a broken tooth, he was glad of company and showed me and allowed me to play with a range of toys that I had never seen. Even now I sometimes wish that I could get back into that pedal-driven racing car of his and see if I couldn't at least break the record for getting down to the corner and back.

• WHOSE LITTLE BOY ARE YOU? •

I was taken to visit the great Douglas Fairbanks and was given, directly from his sacred hands, a prop sword with which he had beaten off hundreds of villainous extras intent on capturing some canvas castle. I was pleased and grateful, but didn't really enjoy it until I could use it to defend my home backyard, where, unfortunately, it came apart in the rains that never fell on Fairbanks' fights in sunny California.

To my mournful satisfaction, the heralded promise of healing was interrupted by a severe case of measles, a case acquired while Elsie and I were in La Jolla in a bungalow overlooking the ocean that I would cross-grainedly have traded for a trudge up the dark stairs of Eighty-fifth Street.

My notion that Ruth and Heywood never wanted to see me again was shaken but not destroyed by Ruth's appearance in La Jolla to help get me through the new illness. Oddly but inevitably she didn't see much of me, spending patient hours reading aloud through the door of the darkened room in which I was confined. (It was believed at the time that light caused severe eye damage to measles patients. I don't know if there was anything in this idea except for the negative evidence that I don't yet wear glasses.)

Shortly after my recovery from the measles began a slow-stages journey back to New York. All I remember of it is the view of Santa Fe's cathedral that one gets while playing about on its steps—a view that makes it seem taller than St. Peter's —and the stark, otherworld, other-century beauty of Taos pueblo at sunset, a vast white community so obviously sensible, self-sufficient, and aesthetically pleasing that all other habitations seemed mean and foolish.

Walking over the rough ground surrounding the pueblo, Ruth sprained her ankle, and in the interests of anesthetic bought from an entrepreneur on the edge of the village a pint of the stuff that was already shaking the community's self-sufficiency, moonshine. In my childlike literalness, I was rather disappointed to discover that a product with such a romantic name was nothing more than a colorless liquid with an acrid smell. It seemed, anyway, to help ease the pain in the ankle.

Returned to New York, I was happy to be back in Lafayette's bed, but between the bouts of illness there, it seemed to me that there were far too many little healthy trips to stay with Elsie MacKnight's parents in the country, one of them extending unforgivably over Christmas.

The why of that Christmas, possibly something perfectly sensible having to do with an infectious illness of Ruth's or Heywood's, lies buried, leaving only a perfectly clear picture of a small boy lying in a strange bed—to be fair, not all that strange—trying to make himself unhappy over neglect while weighing the splendid possibilities in a bulging Christmas stocking that he has just brought upstairs.

I wondered whether Santa had left any additional stuff under the tree in the corner of the Eighty-fifth Street dining room, and I wondered why I wasn't there to find out. The answers are all there somewhere, but the door behind which they lie is warped irretrievably shut, which may be just as well because my own resentful answers were perhaps more gratifying.

My only expression of my feelings about those wretched expeditions was a return to the kind of nastiness that had gummed up Elsie's bag. Once with exhilarating venom, I peeled the bark from a row of young fruit trees in the MacKnight yard, reveling like some mad surgeon in a horror film at the sight of the white sap-sticky flesh I exposed with my pocket knife. It would seem logical to hope that this kind of thing would get you sent home, but the MacKnights, with a patience I found exasperating, continued to put up with my destructive distress signals.

•   •

It was on a winter weekend that the MacKnights were allowed to have to themselves that Ruth, Heywood, and I began
the great adventure in multihouse ownership and occupation
that no one has ever been able satisfactorily to explain. It began
simply enough with Ruth's yearning to get back to the country. She may not have gotten on any too well with her Rogersville relatives, but she missed the fields, the trees, and the
round of the seasons.

The great discovery, or Ruth's idea of a great discovery, was
made on a raw wet day that would have made the Petit Trianon
look forlorn, and neither of the near-collapsed farmhouses on
the favored property had looked, on first viewing, in a class
with the potting sheds of the Trianon farm.

The lands of this Stamford, Connecticut, property were extensive, running to ninety-seven acres, of which eleven were
covered by a shallow lake, but the principal house, almost two
hundred years old when we first saw it, had been built entirely
of wood, and was tired. The hand-hewn beams were works of
art, but the pegs that held them in place had rotted, and the
house sagged so far off the perpendicular that the windows
looked like diamonds. A historical society with lots of money
might have enjoyed restoring it, but it was, in fact, occupied
by a family of squatters with no more money than they got
from the sale of eggs, those produced by the hundred or so
chickens that lived in the house with them.

Creaking and swaying in the December winds that made its
doors work like weeping mouths, it seemed to cry out for some
kind of architectural euthanasia, a bulldozer blow behind the
big stone chimney to send it crashing gratefully to the ground.
The other house was worse. Heywood said that the idea of
buying the place was preposterous and Ruth then said she
would buy it with her own money and he could come as a guest
if he felt like it.

Drunk on the wine of fantasy, she immediately named this

rural wreckage the Sabine Farm after the elegant hideaway that Maecenas, a Roman patron, gave to the poet Horatio some nineteen hundred years before Ruth arrived in Connecticut. Ruth had a little scholarly book called *A Walk to Horace's Farm,* and the text and illustrations indicated that the principal mark of the place was its elegance. It was a full plantation with plenty of farmhands to tend the grapes and serve the resultant wines to Horace and his guests sitting on a terrace overlooking the dark green Sabine hills and the clipped and barbered formal landscape that Horace's staff maintained for the poet's pleasure. It was a place where picnic lunches were laid out on marble tables.

Ruth's farm was more than just thousands of miles from the lands of the ancient Sabini. It looked as Horace's place must have looked after the Goths, Gauls, and Vandals had passed over it several times. Such grapevines as there were wound chokingly and unfruitfully through tangles of scrub shrubbery and the fields, once carefully divided with stone walls, were ragged with evergreen saplings and pimpled with big round volcanic rocks that had rolled off the walls with the well-known willfullness of big round rocks.

There doesn't seem to be any direct reference, in Horace, to poison ivy, although the line, "Naturam expellas furca, tamen usque recurret" (If you drive out nature with a pitchfork, she will soon find a way back), suggests that he knew about noxious weeds, and I hope his farm didn't crust him about with horror as ours did me. It seemed to me that every summer I was at one point carried to the car on a shutter, a swollen mass of suppuration, unwilling to look at a mirror for fear of what I would see, while, in imagination, picturing something that would turn the stomach of Hieronymus Bosch. Taken to New York I would be treated with all the latest nostrums, none of which exist anymore, because none of them were in any way effectual. After awhile I got better as the ailment ran its course, a course it would run again soon.

• WHOSE LITTLE BOY ARE YOU? •

Once Heywood asked for a cure on one of his radio broad-
casts and got more than a hundred and fifty letters, jars, and
bottles. There were also scientific pamphlets from Cornell's
agriculture school. The most romantic of the cures was gun-
powder and cream, the most painful-sounding, kerosene and
sand, but the major message seemed to be that the best thing
was not to touch the leaves. I stayed in the middle of the road
and out of meadows but the result was the same, a fiery, itchy,
oozy blanket of blisters, awful for anyone and especially dam-
aging to a child who had convinced himself that something
dark in his nature was engaged in the spontaneous generation
of poison. I seemed capable also of basting myself with it as
with some demonic pastry brush.

Even today when I smell brown laundry soap—it was supposed to stop the spread of the disease and despite evidence to
the contrary I was constantly bathed in it—I check myself
nervously to see if there are any telltale pinpoint pustules,
although nature, kinder than Horace said it was, does nothing
more these days than lay an occasional red stripe across my
ankles. What was it about the place that appealed to Ruth?
Surely, her father's farm, however unsuccessful, had no resemblance to this barren and neglected place where failure hung
on the burgeoning burdock leaves and the white flag of surrender came out of the milkweed pods that had choked out the
useful crops that had sustained it a century before.

Her explanation was simple, overwhelming, and unsatisfactory. "I wanted it," is all she would ever say. Maybe the answer
was as easy as that it was the only place she could afford. She
was not one for bungalows and handkerchief-patch back gardens. She had a powerful sense of property that rubbed against
Heywood's genial socialism. I think if she had had the money
she would have built a wall around the place.

To add to the feudal flavor of things she even acquired a sort
of vassal in the person of Murdock Pemberton, a press agent,
art critic, and by virtue of hosting the original luncheon, foun-

der of the Algonquin Circle. A handy man with hammer and saw, Murdock was given the tenancy of the second house provided he fixed it up. His son and daughter, Tower and Kate, became my playmates along with John Steinback, a boy from down the road.

"Live undaunted," wrote Horace, "and oppose gallant breaks against the strokes of adversity." The farm was no stranger to the strokes of adversity and Ruth was ready with the gallant breast, buoyed by her delight in a place of her own, a place where she hoped to achieve the deepest and most impossible of her dreams, independence. Stern, unforgiving idealist that she was, she set great store by will. She was unyielding and uncompromising in attitude. When some friend complained to her, probably Murdock, a male chauvinist of deepest dye, whom I think she kept around as a source of good satisfactory arguments, that she had no sense of humor, she put on her sibylline face and raised one eyebrow. "I thank God," she said, "that the dead albatross of a sense of humor has never been hung around my neck."

When, at a party, her old friend James Weldon Johnson, singing "Underneath the Bamboo Tree," got to the line, "I'd like to change your name," she hissed and carried on to the embarrassment of everyone but herself.

Johnson, a distinguished poet and musician, and a leader, with his brother J. Rosamund Johnson, of the black renaissance of the twenties, was also distinguished by a forgiving nature, and he later gave Ruth a copy of his *Book of American Negro Spirituals,* complete with inscription. Indeed there seems to have been a sort of inscribing session with Ruth writing two of her favorite lines on the page opposite the flyleaf and having one of them signed by NAACP secretary Walter White and the other by Julius Bledsoe who sang "Old Man River" in the first production of *Showboat.* The choices were both illustrative of that fanatic quality in Ruth that had led her to hiss her friend.

Walter White put his name beneath "I shall stay—I will stay —and see what the end will be," and Julius Bledsoe endorsed the statement, "If the Deacon's in the way, just roll right over."

When Harold Ross, not yet of *The New Yorker*, had growled at Ruth and his wife Jane Grant as they plotted feminist strategy in his hearing—"For God's sake, why don't you women hire a hall?"—they went out and formed the Lucy Stone League. They didn't, after awhile, have to hire a hall, however, because the house on Eighty-fifth Street was the meeting place for groups planning everything from the most ephemeral theatrical enterprises to that new and better world that the young idealists of that time were so sure they could make.

For all her fanaticism, Ruth exercised a charm that was an effective emollient for the abrasions she dealt out when being what she called forthright and other people called frightening.

From a practical point of view ours was, with the exception of Herbert Swope's inconveniently distant castle at Sands Point, the largest establishment in the Algonquin group. Mattie could improvise a dinner with ten or fifteen minutes' notice, and our cellar, if that's the right description for a plentiful supply of gin, stood ready to fuel any conference that was beginning to flag.

For Ruth and Heywood, uneasy with intimacies—those exposures of the parts of oneself that must for good and scary reasons be kept hidden—the waves of people washing through the house or lying agreeably stranded in the guest room were useful diversions. For Heywood the rhythm-band sounds of rattling voices, clinking glasses, and occasional musical counterpoint were usually sufficient to keep his fears quiet, if not to kill them; but for Ruth, much as she liked the jolly parliament over which she presided, there was sometimes a need for the silence of aloneness. This was where the country house came in.

Ruth was going to roll right over the difficulties she had

acquired with the purchase of her decayed demesne. The Sabine Farm was going to be her castle, her retreat, the place where her weariness would not be that of frustration but, she hoped, just the honest exhaustion that comes from making a house stand straight again.

From the beginning it was clear, too, that only one device, hers, would emblazon any banners on that castle.

In a big feminist gesture Heywood had managed to get her name on the deed of the Eighty-fifth Street house, listed as belonging to "Heywood Broun and Ruth Hale, his wife," but there was no return gesture from Ruth. She had offered him a chance to buy it, probably aware that he would not see its possibilities, and now the place was all hers, with its pond immediately named Hale Lake.

Work began on the Sabine farmhouse as soon as the weather was warm enough for the chickens and their proprietors to move out without hardship, and the first work was further destruction.

Like most New England farmhouses, this one had been divided into innumerable very small rooms, some so tiny that body heat alone would bring the temperature up to some bearable level. The heating system was a fireplace and a collection of oil stoves venting through a lot of tin pipes in the walls. That the place had not burned down in the 190 years since a Mr. Holly had built it for his young wife and the son who was later to live in Murdock's house was against every probability.

Step one in the renovation was the removal of a majority of the cell-dividing walls. With an understanding smile, Ruth began the new era by handing Heywood a pickax, aware as she was of all the violence that was storing up in the big shy man who worked so hard at being lovable.

"I'll bet you've been wanting to do this for a long time," she said, and with a happy explosion Heywood disappeared into a cloud of falling plaster and splintering lath.

• WHOSE LITTLE BOY ARE YOU? •

When the junked walls were at last hauled away, the first of the two floors consisted of a living room and a medium-sized bedroom. Cooking was done in a sort of shed built around the wellhead and fastened to the back wall of the living room. Mattie said it reminded her of the place she had come north to escape, but she managed to make do in it even after a summer storm had thrown a lightning bolt at the iron stove and nearly knocked her down the well.

Upstairs there were six bedrooms arranged around a stairwell and their combined weight soon produced a sag in the ceiling of the living room, now no longer supported by all those interior walls.

Experts were summoned who installed a lot of hidden ironwork, so that although the house still looked like the old New England in excelsis, with its hand-hewn beams and wideboard flooring, it was actually a wood-veneered Erector set.

These unexpected expenditures on supports for the house were enough to make plumbing a dream of the future, and enough additional problems showed up in the first few years to defer the dream more than once. I'm not sure that Murdock didn't have a bathroom before we did, although I'm sure we were too proud to cross the meadow dividing the two houses and beg for its use.

Ruth was impatient for the pleasures of proprietorship and by the middle of the first summer, though much was lacking, she had moved in and begun receiving guests, among the first of whom was Dorothy Parker, hoping that a little country quiet would help her through a spell of medically recommended abstinence from alcohol. Also there was the actor Ed MacNamara, a perfect guest who could manage to find and provide entertainment in a lifeboat.

Among the unwanted guests in the house were a bunch of rats who had been drawn there by the easy pickings among the chickens and who were now suffering severe withdrawal symptoms.

Mac and Ruth, chatting with Mrs. Parker in a friendly half circle around the fireplace, had accumulated a supply of bread pills that they would from time to time quietly toss toward the walls. The famished rats, some of them gaunt but still quite big from the happy old days of plenty, would come rushing out to these hors d'oeuvres with quite a display of scrabbling claws and flashing eyes.

Mrs. Parker—in the middle of something like "Then Deems Taylor went to the piano and"—would freeze. Ruth and Mac, affecting not to notice the vigorous invasion, would politely urge her to go on. At about the time she got to what George Kaufman had said about what Deems had played, they would roll out a little more bread and there would be more pouncing and munching.

Mrs. Parker, almost convinced by the smiling calm of her companions that the rats were no more than proof of the arrival of the pink elephant phase of her problem, finally nerved herself after a particularly grumbly–greedy performance to say in a tight, even voice, "Does anyone but myself see giant rats in this room?"

It had been the original plan to say, "What rats, Dottie?" but a look at the fragile face, a gardenia petal bruised by fear, was too much for the plotters, and they showed her how the ghastly spectacle was triggered. It was probably a place for one of her famous put-downs, but the best she could manage was a simple, heartfelt "You sons of bitches!"

•   •

Many years after this first adventurous summer at the farm, Marc Connelly, as the last surviving chief of the Algonquin tribe, and I, as a relative of departed members, were at a publicity party for a television film about the good days when wit was only ten cents a pound. We got to talking about Mac-Namara, and a young press agent who knew all about Dorothy

Parker, George Kaufman, and the other headliners of the group drew me aside to murmur, "Who was this MacNamara that you and Mr. Connelly are talking about?"

The sharp-eared Connelly heard him and, turning his great round baby face on the questioner and coughing a little to focus attention, proclaimed, "Ed MacNamara was the greatest container of love and affection that I ever met."

There are many stories that the dwindling band of Mac's admirers cherish but if you put them all together and analyze the mass, the answer will turn up in Marc's words. Because Mac was always so ready to give, he ended up receiving in overflowing measure. He had studied the art of "guesting" with the painstaking care that other artists give to the violin or the creation of perfect Alexandrines. He could make himself indispensable within an hour of his unexpected arrival at your house.

The kitchen facilities of Ruth's farm being below chuck wagon standards, you would imagine that a large party would do well to eat before arrival; but Mac solved that with his famed magic steaks, hundreds of which he could prepare rapidly over a primitive grill, each piece of meat being wrapped in a little individual oven made of damp salt and wet paper napkins. Only Mac knew how to do this so that the unstable elements successfully adhered, and he could pour a few drinks and sing a few songs while the meat was cooking.

When the cooking was over and the last crust thrown into the fire, he would, in his resonant singer's voice, tell stories, wrapping them up as neatly as he had done the pieces of meat and timing them like the great conductors under whose batons he had never quite managed to sing. I suppose one of the things that Ruth and Heywood, that driven pair, found fascinating about Mac was his lack of drive. A childhood more than usually full of disappointment had made him decide to be a survivor rather than a striver. He had tried as a boy to be unnaturally good, good enough to achieve a position as an altar boy in the church.

"For a whole year I had no fun," he used to say. "And when at last the priest told me I had made it, he said I should get my mother to give me a dollar for the surplice. She didn't have the dollar and I got turned down for the job. Oh, I never went into the place again!"

In the poor Irish neighborhoods of Paterson, New Jersey, where there wasn't a dollar to fulfill the ambitions of piety, there often wasn't a dollar to buy dinner; and the young Mac-Namara, turning from the spiritual to the practical, made regular dinners his principal desire in life. It was probably with the thought of a steady if stodgy life that he joined the Paterson police force, a job for which he was totally unsuited in every way except appearance, which was of a casting director's compleat cop—square red face, bright blue eyes, and all.

In his subsequent theatrical career he was invariably cast as a policeman, although once he told me with some pleasure that he was being cast outside the force. "It's a Civil War play by Lloyd Lewis," he told me cheerily, and then his face fell. "Of course, wouldn't you know it, I'm in the Union army and have to wear a blue uniform."

That the harshness of his early life had narrowed his horizons was not surprising, but that it had created a creature overflowing with fun and kindness was very surprising indeed. His measure is to be found perhaps in his sad, soft record in the police proceedings of a tough town.

In all his years as a beat cop he never, no matter how anarchic or unruly the situation with which he dealt, arrested anyone. His sole act of violence was the killing of a "mad" dog.

"It was a poor little thing, foaming at the mouth from nothing more than the terrible heat of a Paterson summer. I had my orders and did what I had to, missing the first shot because I couldn't stand to look at what I was doing. On the way back to the station I threw my gun in the river and never carried one again."

Ruth, who wanted to change herself and the world, and Heywood, who, apparently despairing of himself, was going to give full time to building a better world, must have felt wonderfully relaxed sitting around with Mac—a real Irishman who with heightened effects had become a stage Irishman and whose big ambition was to stay at our house until Harold Ross got back from wherever and could take him in until he got a play or went to stay awhile with his great friend James Cagney.

I played a small part in the only live television show Cagney ever did. When we were seated in a circle, the director began the ritual of introducing us to the star. When he identified me, Cagney said in his soft, rapid voice, "Heywood Broun, Heywood Broun," and I waited for the business about how he had known my father. "Mr. Broun," he said, "you were a friend of Ed MacNamara. You know, that may be our immortality, yours and mine, that we were friends of Ed MacNamara."

Much is made in pop sociology circles about the age of self-expression and self-satisfaction that has made thinking of others almost a kind of unhealthy denial of one's identity, but it occurs to me that Mac managed to take care of a great many people in the process of seeing to his own pleasures.

I remember, for example, a Christmas that was running down, littered with tissue wrappings and greasy with turkey dressing. It was sliding toward surfeit and sullenness when Mac appeared in the doorway and, addressing a small boy, waved aloft a pair of passes to the traditional Christmas-night hockey game between the New York Rangers and the New York Americans. "Here is half of your Christmas present," said Mac, who had probably winkled the pair out of a sportswriter at the Players' Club bar.

"What's the other half?" I asked. "Ah, that's the best part," said Mac. "I go with you and explain the game to you." We both had a splendid time and I'm sure that even the sportswriter was left with a glow as a result of some skillful lie of Mac's in which he said he was taking a crippled orphan to the game who would bless the writer's name while there was breath in his twisted little body.

In a competitive world, Mac seemed never to pass anybody in any races. Like some saintly marathon runner, he was always stopping to give out cups of water, words of wisdom, or the words of some song you had always wanted to learn.

His singing ambitions in youth had never much extended beyond filling in with Irish folk songs while Madame Ernestine Schumann-Heink, whose protege he was, gathered her venerable energies for penultimate, ultimate, and postultimate assaults on "Die Erlkoenig," the great horror song with which she could chill your blood even after her rendering sounded like the work of a talented frog.

For a brief stretch, Mac decided he should try to be more than a backup singer and applied himself to lessons, one of them an informal coaching session with Caruso. The ambition wafted away very shortly, carried off by the laughter at one of his jokes or wreathed in the smoke from one of his steak-cooking fires. But he saved some wisdom that, as usual, he passed on to the rest of us, in this case Caruso's simple secret of successful singing.

"Mac," he had said, "you know whatta you do when you shit? Singing, it's the same thing, only Up!"

I thought of Mac, as I thought of all grown-ups, as being without fear. What, after all, did they have to be afraid of, having survived the terrors of childhood?

I was, therefore, deeply shocked on the only occasion when my hero was obviously afraid. It was at dinner at our house and he was well launched in one of his anti-Catholic diatribes. Sitting across from him was Frank Sullivan, the only genuinely sweet-natured wit I ever met, and in the middle of some "Sin of the Scarlet Woman of Rome," Frank picked a piece of bread out of a basket in the center of the table and began to mutter his way through the Mass, elevating the bread as the Host when the occasion came.

Mac's square ruddy face became pale and almost trapezoidal. Its normal jollity twisted into zigzags of fear, and in a high strained voice he said, "Frank, cut that out. Stop right now."

Frank smiled gently—obviously his mother had had enough money for the surplice—and replaced the bread in the basket. "When you can remain calm at such a performance," he told Mac, "you'll be entitled to finish that speech."

Later I found out that Frank was pathologically afraid of travel and that his only extended journey had been a train ride to St. Louis when he was exhibited to a psychiatric convention by the doctor who had nursed him through the trip.

At the time, though, I was mad at him, a worry-free grown-up, for upsetting Mac. I loved Mac all the more for sharing a weakness with me. He was one of two outside grown-ups with whom I felt the warmth of loving and being loved. The other, a person who had every right to be afraid of a genuinely unfair world, was Paul Robeson. In the years in which I knew him and worshipped him, he faced that world with a rumbling and confident joy.

Heywood had met Paul during the run of Eugene O'Neill's *Emperor Jones* at the Provincetown Playhouse, and he became one of the regulars in the group that came to our house after being someplace else, before going someplace else, or for the whole evening because they weren't going anyplace else.

I first heard him sing at one of our giant New Year's Eve parties. Those affairs packed the first floor, denuded of furniture and filled with folding chairs from which, at midnight, everyone jumped into the New Year. (The custom has disappeared since any group of more than five who simultaneously

jumped to the floor of a modern New York building would end
up in the cellar.)

There were usually about two hundred guests at these parties and the logistics of serving might have been a problem if
it had not been early decreed that food is a nuisance at a big
gathering and Prohibition liquor other than gin was dangerous.
Everything of a refreshing nature, therefore, came from a big,
constantly recharged vat of gin and orange juice over which,
upon the arrival of 1924, I presided.

Heywood was away in the early part of the evening and
Ruth promised me that I could stay up as late as I liked, expecting me, I suppose, to drop over early. She forgot that a child
who is the center of attention as I—ladle in hand, certainly was
—will stay awake through tiredness and on into the strange,
precollapse clarity of exhaustion.

The task of serving was not difficult, since the sloppings
went back into the big bowl, and I reveled in the knowledge
that I was, in fact, the master of the revels. I forget exactly
when Heywood got home, but it was at an hour when few
small children were still up, and horrified at discovering me
still at my job of pouring energy into the guests, he ordered me
at once to bed. I pointed out that Ruth had said I could stay
up as late as I wanted and that I felt fine. With the kind of ugly
logic that grown-ups produce on these occasions, he pointed
out that he had promised me nothing and that his order was
for immediate retirement. To cover my retreat, I entered a plea
that increasingly had been used as a palliative for the pains of
discipline.

"Let Paul tell me to go to bed," I asked, and Paul was duly
brought to the refreshment table and gave me the command,
accompanying it with a smile of loving complicity, but a smile
that made it all right to be suddenly very sleepy and rather glad
that I didn't have to dispense any more of the stuff that smelled
like hard candy dissolved in after-shave. I thankfully climbed

the stairs to oblivion, buoyed by Paul's promise that if I missed anything he would tell me all about it the next time he saw me.

A year later, planning a larger part for myself in the New Year gala, I got turned down on staying up at my option, but I was promised that Paul would come up at about quarter to twelve and wake me so that I could be present at least at the magic moment.

When, as it worked out, I woke up on the morning of January 1, after an unbroken night's sleep, I was furious at Ruth and Heywood. I dismissed as unbelievable their explanation that Paul had, in fact, tried to wake me up, and had done everything short of such dangerous shock tactics as immersing me in cold water, without effect. I was then, as I was to be for many years, so inwardly terrified at the blazing violence of my anger that I simply walked out of the room and retreated into the safe passivity of sullen silence. After a day in which a small zombie wandered the house accepting food but not comfort or communication, a message reached Paul and he came on a sort of hurt-feelings house call and told me the same story I had already heard. I instantly believed it because he was so transparently guileless and good. I recalled some occasions when fire engines in the street had not brought me to the surface, and everything was settled with his promise that the following year he would, if necessary, drop me in the tub.

If MacNamara was the greatest container for love and affection, then Paul was, of all the people I have met, the greatest dispenser of them.

When he said hello to you for the first time, you were at once aware that he was vastly taken with you. After you had spoken with him for a few minutes you realized that he was finding your wonderful hidden qualities, and after a few more meetings you were trying to think of ways to tell him how much he meant to you.

Many years later when I took a college roommate to see Paul

in a not very good show called *John Henry*, we visited backstage
for a few minutes and after we left, the roommate, a rather
reserved and brooding scholarly type, said suddenly, "I'd like
to jump off a ship to retrieve something Paul Robeson dropped
overboard."

It was at one of the New Year's parties that Heywood suggested to Paul that he give a concert of the songs he had been
doing informally at friends' houses. Paul protested that the
spirituals he sang were fairly simple musical fare, that he had
no formal voice training, and that you could hear the songs for
nothing by visiting any church in Harlem.

"You hire the hall," said Heywood, "and we'll provide the
audience."

By "we" Heywood meant the Algonquin crowd, more particularly those who had a forum, and most particularly his
colleagues on the opposite editorial page of the *World.* These
included Frank Adams, whose "Conning Tower" column was
signed "F.P.A."; Alexander Woollcott; Deems Taylor, the
World's music critic; and playwright-columnist Laurence Stallings, co-author of the play *What Price Glory?*

Paul arranged to take the Provincetown on the *Emperor*'s
night off, and Paul's friends began their campaign. By the date
of the concert the word was all over smart New York that
anyone who failed to hear this new young singer had missed
out on the music event of the year. Crowds swirled in the street
in front of the small theater and offered lucky ticket holders
very large sums to give up their seats. Heywood had kept his
promise, but the triumph, of course, was Paul's because by the
time his big easy voice had boomed happily to the end of his
last joyous song, the promise of the musical event of the year
had also been kept.

Heywood used to say that his largest contribution to American culture might turn out to be his persuasion of Giants'
manager John McGraw not to turn the young Christy Math-

ewson into a first baseman. Maybe McGraw wouldn't have so misused a great pitcher anyway, and maybe somebody else would soon have persuaded Paul to a concert, but I am proud for Heywood and happy for Paul.

I still have a record of Paul singing "Sometimes I Feel like a Motherless Child," with a little paper label pasted on it that says, "For Woodie, hoping he will never feel so."

The last time I saw Paul he sang to thousands of American soldiers in the bomb-scarred Nuremberg Opera House. He sang the songs of uncomplicated faith that he had always sung, and to the dismay of the brass, he sang the defiant songs of the Loyalists of the Spanish Civil War. There in the ruins of beauty and very possibly the wreckage of the world's hopes, he rallied us, one strong voice telling us that the Battle of Jericho would be won and that the four insurgent generals would, in the end, fail.

I embraced him after the concert, and I wished then in the confusion and terrors of war, as I was going to in many confusions and terrors after that, that I could go up to bed at Paul's command with the knowledge that he would shortly wake me for something wonderful.

Paul was among the few people about whom the members of the Algonquin Round Table or Circle or whatever you wanted to call this curious confederation, agreed. The picture of the "Algonks," as some called them, that now seems to exist among cultural archaeologists and seekers of the lost road to sophistication is of a group that spoke in a single voice tuned to high purpose and high good humor. They were supposed to be somehow aware that future generations would look back on them in awe.

In fact, of course, they were a bunch of small-town young people trying to make a name in the big town. True, they eventually made their boisterousness born of uneasiness into a kind of stylishness, and true, their clinging together created among them the kind of warmth that is engendered by the singsongs and riddle sessions that lifeboat commanders organize to keep people from thinking about sharks.

After all, the Founding Fathers didn't know they were going to end up on stamps and money and insurance company posters any more than the little group of Welsh adventurers who got together with old Uther's son Arthur to carve out a little lebensraum knew that someday they would be in the musical comedy *Camelot*.

The members of the circle would have—and some of them did—traded any hope of a place in posterity for the comforting sound of impermanent laughter, the approval of those around the Table. An awful lot of things didn't get written because the potential writer was working on a joke that could be passed off as spontaneous wit. Certainly at the beginning, they were strangely innocent, oddly square, and about as worldly as Booth Tarkington's seventeen-year-old Willie Baxter.

Because he had been born in New York and had been to Harvard, Heywood was the Talleyrand of the Table, his views on *smart* or *not smart* eagerly sought by people who were just wise enough not to ask him questions about matters of dress.

Consider the atmosphere of the famous Thanatopsis Literary and Inside Straight Club, the poker-playing auxiliary of the Algonquin Circle, and how much The TL and IS resembled the average game down at the firehouse or the Legion hall.

The men and occasional women around the green baize board were for the most part certified wits, but wit is an exhausting business and so is poker, and it was perhaps with relief that the players laughed at such wheezes as folding a stud hand burdened with the two lowest cards in the deck while remarking "I have been trey-deuced." George S. Kaufman, master of comedy, is credited with this mild joke, which he trotted out again and again along with his other number nifty, "I shall fold my tens like the Arabs and silently steal away."

When Raoul Fleischmann, financial founder and publisher of *The New Yorker*, assembled a royal flush, passersby in the second-floor corridor of the Algonquin could have heard from the poker room much alehouse laughter over the repeated addressing of remarks to "Royal Flushman."

The club was named for a group that appeared in Sinclair Lewis' *Main Street*—"And of course there's our women's study club—The Thanatopsis Club . . . they've made the city plant ever so many trees, and they run the rest rooms for farmer's wives. And they do take such an interest in refinement and culture. So—in fact, so very unique."

The game had begun, according to Frank Adams, at an apartment shared by Harold Ross and John T. Winterich, ex-members of the staff of the AEF publication *Stars and Stripes*. Adams, who as a captain had been the CO of the paper, was there as well as Woollcott and Heywood.

Later it filled up with celebrities like Harpo Marx, Kaufman, and Herbert Swope, foreman of all the writers in the New York *World*'s corral but—as George Eliot wanted everyone who read *Adam Bede* to smell fresh hay—it was impossible to be around that game as I was as a small kibitzer without getting at least a whiff of the cracker-barrel from all these outland adventurers who, in the working hours, were the arbiters of sophistication in the American arts. They had more rituals than a nineteenth-century lodge. They rose to their feet when bad play was detected and chanted, to the tune of Gilbert and Sullivan's "He remains an Englishman," a condemnatory, "He remains a goddamned fool."

The theatrical press agent John Toohey was always addressed as "Our Founder," and always rose and bowed when so addressed. From time to time after some remark deemed appropriate to the tag, they would all chant "As the Girl Said to the Sailor," punch line of a wartime dirty story—just the sort of thing Chum Frink, George Babbitt, and all the Sinclair

Lewis characters the club found amusing would find amusing.

Naturally, such a group produced a good deal of better stuff than that before the onset of what Adams called "Winners' Sleeping Sickness" or "Losers' Insomnia or Broun's Disease," but what struck me was the relief with which they put off, with their jackets, the burdens of being bright, and relaxed into the undemanding joys of frat house fun.

My share in the latter consisted of playing straight child to Heywood in a routine that went, "I was at the zoo today, Woodie."

"Say, did you see any interesting animals?"

"Yes, there were two fascinating ox-like beasts and as I stood between their cages I was reminded of a cigar."

"Oh, what cigar?"

"Between the Yaks."

Later when one of the beasts got up, he was reminded of a song "Mighty Yak A Rose." I guess it was not much of an interest in refinement and culture, and as the stakes inevitably rose, the coziness sank until—Thanatopsis, after all, means the contemplation of death—members of the game contemplating their own ruin quietly withdrew, leaving a changed and genuinely sophisticated group of rich players to take the chips and their chances out to Swope's house at Sands Point, the place Scott Fitzgerald used as a model for Gatsby's house.

For the erstwhile rubes who had found for awhile some echo of their cheerfully undemanding pasts, it was back to the production of plays, pamphlets, pictures—all the things that would have gone unappreciated back from 'where they came.

Ruth was a forceful conversationalist and appears to have done a lot of talking at early Algonquin gatherings. She was at that time a country girl who had arrived. All traces of Tennessee had been trimmed away from her speech and she was unforgiving of the deviations that so many of us throw, like beer cans or sandwich wrappers, on the language of Shakespeare. She growled at the radio when announcers in search of gentility told us that some program would be heard "This afternyoon," or urged us "To send in the cyoopon in order to receive a free toob" of something or other. Heywood never stopped referring to officers of the law as "pleecemen," and she never stopped correcting him.

Ruth marshaled her words as carefully as she pronounced them, and in Frank Case's Rose Room she was listened to not only because of her powers of expression, but because her accomplishments aroused awe in those who were still hoping to hear from this or that publisher, producer, or press agent about the job that would keep things going until hope and circumstances met.

I suppose her most remarkable credential was her World War I service as editor of a Paris-based edition of the Chicago *Tribune.* That a young woman should be appointed to such a post in the faraway sexist days of 1917, when the only apparent jobs for the "fair sex" were patting white pillows in a hospital or distributing white feathers in the streets, is extraordinary. Like the other extraordinary things in Ruth's early life, it was never explained to me, but simply stated as a fact and adorned, occasionally, with anecdote.

• •

Heywood Broun and Ruth Hale, his wife, sailed for France the day after they were married, he as a correspondent for the New York *Tribune.* Still tolerant of the social conventions that ensnared her husband, Ruth had consented, on the way to the boat, to stop in at what she described as "a drugstore jewelry counter" and pick up a wedding ring that would make their double-name hotel registration a little more acceptable. After a month in Paris, however, she pointed out that the concierge of the large cold penthouse apartment in which they were based seemed to take no interest in their status, and that the ring was, in fact, no more than a badge of servitude. Its useful end, announced Ruth, would be its deposit in one of the many charity boxes posted around Paris for the benefit of war widows, women economically handicapped in a society that had no work for them after taking away their husbands.

Heywood reluctantly agreed, but suggested that sensibility might be served if the ring were melted into a nugget. He argued that the widows charged with opening the boxes might be affected by the sight of proof that still another dear one was lost.

In order to achieve this disguise they put the ring in a frying pan and held it over the small open fire that was their sole source of heat. For some time nothing happened and they filled the lull with discussions of the silliness or nonsilliness of what they were doing, but at last there was an audible pop in the pan, and the ring separated into a small pool of gilt and a blackened circle of some unknown metal. Ruth at once announced that it was deeply satisfying to discover that the ring was as counterfeit as the custom that had created it; but in order that the widows shouldn't suffer from the fraud, they made a small cash contribution in one of the boxes.

In France the paths of their careers made that inexplicable divergence that saw him pass and eclipse her, even as he depended more and more on her help and criticism.

If prizes were given for sheer dint, Ruth would have been winner. It must have been a tremendous job to put together a paper in wartime Paris, even a weekly as this was. At the best of times French printing was as full of typos as a bouillabaisse is of shell bits. Given the handicap of the English language with its baffling spelling, the French typographers must have given Mlle. Éle a difficult time. Still, she seemed to get on with them as their chief invited her home one Sunday to his family dinner, assuring her that she would be served *un plat tout à fait Americain, mice.* She was relieved to discover that the dish was, in fact, maize, little tasteless ears thereof, whose overcooked state was proof that *mice* was a *plat tout à fait Americain.*

Ruth rarely discussed her time in France, although in one of Alec Woollcott's letters there is the line, "She [Ruth] herself has been far nearer the front than I and can tell you many things I have never seen and may never see." Whether Ruth ever called on Mrs. Alice Truax, recipient of the letter, and told her all those things, I don't know. She was oddly silent about the whole business with me.

I think those days in France were the last in which she felt in control of her own destiny and therefore happy in the enjoyment of that independence so fiercely wanted and yet so easily defeated.

The baby conceived in the apartment on the Boulevard Raspail and born in New York on March 10, 1918, was a distraction for which she wasn't and never would be prepared. I was her gift to Heywood, who wanted a son for all the usual wrong reasons. They were considerations of dynasty, fertility, masculinity, things that are satisfied on the day the child is born, leaving one with all the subsequent years in which, not having really wanted a small playmate, one didn't know what to do with him.

Despite my wheeze about making me eligible for the presidency, I think it was grumblings from the army about Mr. Broun's eccentricities that made them come home.

Heywood's pieces in the *Tribune* had been popular and successful, so much so that they were gathered into books called *The AEF* and *Our Army at the Front,* and were, in the early days of the American involvement, full of cheerful sporting metaphor. He wrote pieces about how doughboys got sore arms from throwing hand grenades with a baseball pitching motion; and he wrote a story about how General Pershing, passing through a mess hall, had noticed a KP pausing in the act of potato peeling to look worshipfully up at his commander in chief. "Take that man's name," Pershing had barked, breaking a heart without breaking a stride.

Comparing Black Jack to the paternally nicknamed Maréchal Joffre, always "Papa" to his poilus, Heywood wrote, "They will never call him Papa Pershing," and when the *Tribune* thought of sending him back after the respite in the States, the army made it clear that they would prefer another correspondent.

Of course, they may have objected to his habit of wearing a fedora hat instead of an officer's cap with his correspondent's uniform, or the general dishevelment of that uniform, bought at the Galeries Lafayette department store, an outfit that led one exasperated major at an inspection of correspondents to ask fretfully, "Mr. Broun, have you fallen down?"

•   •

Heywood Campbell Broun, the big young man with his gaping Sam Browne belt and his wrong-way-around puttees, was a startling (and secretly satisfying) contrast to his father, the picture soldier, Major Heywood Cox Broun of the National Guard. The latter should be seen on his way to one of the many meets in which, as one of the top pistol marksmen in the country, he would compete. He would be in perfect uniform and display perfection in his martial art.

Perhaps Heywood Hale Broun was foolish to be afraid of Heywood Campbell Broun, that gentle fearful man, but no one could blame a gentle fearful man for being afraid of Heywood Cox Broun.

My grandfather was, in his own terms, perfect. I never met a person so completely without guilt or self-examination, so sure that his world was the best of all possible ones, largely because he had been so skilled and wise in making it so.

One of three poor Scottish brothers, scions of one of the oldest and most undistinguished families in the annals of British genealogy, he arrived in this country at the age of twelve with his belongings in the traditional handkerchief at the end of a stick. He saw one brother off to Australia and wealth, the other off to Brooklyn and anonymity. Then, like some Horatio Alger, he rose rapidly through the ranks at a printing firm, headed it before he was thirty, sold it, and started the second assault on America. Having achieved prosperity, he wanted a place in society. Looking over the narrow list of occupations open to gentlemen, he chose to be a wine merchant. With ink still on his fingers, he applied himself to the study of the ornamentation of fashionable life. In no time at all he could tell you after a sniff or a sip the year and provenance of any wine and whether it had been properly stored. A bite told him the feeding habits of the pheasant, which was now part of *his* feeding habit. Long after his death, his son was to be deferred to in restaurants of quality on grounds having nothing to do with his own celebrity, but because of his connection with a man to whom a menu was invitation to achievement in the way a keyboard was to Paderewski. On such occasions my father would often childishly and willfully break all the rules, demanding claret with his clams and a mixture of vinaigrette dishes and cream sauce confections that would make the captain cry out in protest.

"I know what I want," Heywood would say firmly, wanting, in fact, to deny the domination of the man who was *always right.*

Yet when Heywood gave a reconciliation dinner for Alec Woollcott after one of the spats that were inevitable between Alec and his friends, he amazed the maitre d' by planning a beautifully balanced menu in the best nineteenth-century tradition of stylish stuffing.

For 800 years no Broun in the long line of soldiers, sheep counters, notaries, and country lawyers in the Lowlands town of Colston had accomplished anything worthy of note.

Heywood was fond of pointing out, to his father's annoyance, that the only Broun in literature was to be found in Sir Walter Scott's *Heart of Midlothian.* This Jessie Broun was "A woman no better than she should be." Indeed, the family's distinction was a negative one. So many Brouns had served Louis XI, the Spider King of France, in his Scottish Archer Guard that he gave the family the right to wear the fleur de lis on their coat of arms. The family motto, "Floreat Majestas," Let Majesty Flourish, has the proper broken-backed sound for a bunch who found none of Louis' awful errands too awful.

One family problem that still persists surfaced in this time when Brouns were running over the Spider King's webs in his dreadful service and appears in the King's records. No one except an actual member of the undistinguished little Clan Broun can spell the name correctly. This led, according to a historial footnote I read, to a lot of trouble at the pay table as ancestors found themselves lost under Braun, Brown, Brun, or even occasionally and inexplicably, Boom. As every old soldier knows, if *they* make a mistake, *you* pay for it, and as I struggle late at night to get a hotel computer to confess my reservation, I feel at one with those old rascals protesting to some unyielding French bureaucrat that they'll sign any name he wants if he'll just disgorge the wage.

Heywood once tried to cut this Gordian knot by changing the spelling to Broon, but his father was suddenly very huffy about the traditions of the family and even hinted that a name change might rot the magic pear on which, according to legend, our fortunes depend. It seems that a medieval Broun married the daughter of a wizard who presented the young couple with the fruit and announced that Brouns would flourish while it was preserved. If you don't believe in wizards, this just seems like a cheap gift, but our annals record that a subsequent Lady Broun who just dreamed about losing the pear lost most of her family in a boating accident, and when last heard of, the pear existed "a wizened vegetable curiosity" in a glass case somewhere. Either the pear or grandfather frightened Heywood into submission, and we are still giving the five simple letters to people who get three or four of them right—the name of Scotland's dullest family. Our most fiery ancestor gave his whole life to a campaign to make white-tie mandatory with evening kilts.

Unexpectedly this uninspiring heritage produced that blossom of excellence and elegance, Heywood Cox Broun, mighty marksman, a champion at such arcane and difficult forms of billiards as Black Pin and Balkline, an overachiever and a charmer.

Even Ruth, who knew that her father-in-law subscribed to the old notion that "Men are God's tree and women are his flowers," found him irritatingly irresistible. She told me that she gave way to the family desire that I be named Heywood because of his pleas at a luncheon. He had paid her the compliment of ignoring his usual nineteenth-century custom of ordering the food without consulting his presumably ignorant female guest, and amused her by offering to give a hundred dollars toward the upbringing of a properly named grandchild.

"If he had offered some big sum I would have been angry," she said, "but the bribe was so small and silly that I laughed and then he laughed, and before I knew it, you were Heywood Broun III. I wonder whether he knew that was the way it would turn out."

He was still alive and I suspect a little annoyed when his grandson came down to breakfast one day and announced, "From now on I'm not Heywood Broun III, I am Heywood Hale Broun."

Children are always saying, "From now on I'm Duke, or Flash, or Esmeralda, or Myfanwy," but usually it only lasts a week. My change, obviously, stuck, and when the passport office, having forgotten what a nuisance the Hales were, gave me a document with the three names, despite the fact that only two occur on my birth certificate, it was forever official. (I don't know why I didn't originally get a full load of names like the two previous Heywoods, the second of whom actually was Matthew Heywood Campbell Broun.)

As a means of pleasing Ruth it was first-rate, but as a means of changing my identity, it was as ramshackle a gesture as one could imagine, and often leads now to my being called Heywood Hale Broun, Jr.

If someone had pointed out to Heywood Cox Broun that he was totally self-concerned and remarkably ungiving in emotional matters, he would have laughed comfortably and pointed out that his wife had a butler, a cook, and two housemaids, and that his children attended the best schools, proof positive that he was the best of husbands and fathers.

He was, of course, one of the best-dressed men in New York and knew every answer in the complicated game of proper attire for all occasions. With a mixture of envy and affection Heywood told me that when, in his youth, he received invitations, he always went to his father, who would ask the address and a few questions about the host or hostess, then tent his fingertips like Mycroft Holmes, and, like Holmes, come up with an answer correct to the texture of the shoelaces. This story suggests that there must have been a time when Heywood was well dressed or at least trying so to be. Later, however, he attained attention as the worst-dressed man in New York. Like his father, he liked to be at the head of the parade whichever way it was marching.

When his father died Heywood summed him up as one "who took and gave much joy in life" and compared him to Thackeray's Colonel Newcome, that grand old man whose death caused his creator to weep. Then, unable to go all that far, Heywood remarked that his father had "just a dash" of another Thackeray character, Major Pendennis, perhaps secure in the knowledge that nobody read Thackeray anymore and wouldn't know that the major was a vain buck with a vast knowledge of forks, cravats, and the social genealogy of placement at table.

I have a photo of my grandfather standing in a row of fashionables at the opening of the Greentree tennis court in 1915. I look a good deal like the man in the picture and still wonder why he didn't think his nose was too big, when I spent years concealing mine behind my hand.

The youth who was anxious not to wear black-tie to a white-tie party finally went to a dinner at Mrs. William Randolph Hearst's in a tailcoat belonging to MacNamara, who was six or seven inches shorter than he. Between Mac's vest and Heywood's trousers there was a gap of flesh that Heywood concealed by remaining in a deferential crouch or bow, a pose that led Mrs. Norman de R. Whitehouse to tell Frank Adams that Broun was one of the most courtly men she had ever met.

Someone, probably Alec Woollcott, said that Heywood looked like an unmade bed and Heywood made sure that the remark got around, adding to his messiness myth with occasional columns in which he discussed such things as "Why I am not a well-dressed man."

"I am what I am without premeditation," he wrote mendaciously. "Never have I planned to look any way in particular. And taking a thought about clothes seems to me a little contemptible. Beau Brummell is not worthy of emulation."

Take that, Heywood Cox Broun!

When my grandfather took a beating in the stock market, the one place where he was not always right, he would send to London for a dozen made-to-measure silk shirts as proof that his confidence was unimpaired even though his bank balance was battered.

I am perhaps the only person who knew that Heywood really thought that both Brummell and his father were achingly worthy of emulation, and that he simply lacked the confidence that hung around the old gentleman like a discreet cologne.

The occasion of my discovery was the arrival of a suit Heywood had had made for him by his father's traditional tailor. I sat in a corner watching as he unpacked it, looked at it with the pleasure of a child inspecting an inspired Halloween costume, and then with a care Brummell would have approved, put it on. Before going to the mirror he fiddled the knot of his tie into a dimpled perfection, and when he arrived at the glass he had a military bearing, a proud carriage Pershing never saw, but that did wonders for Heywood and for the new suit.

Looking past him into the mirror I saw a tall, admittedly heavy man of considerable elegance and address. Heywood saw the same image and for a moment smiled approvingly at himself, for a moment permitted himself a taste of sartorial self-esteem. At that moment he could have walked into some mahogany-leathery club lounge arm in arm with his father, a couple of men about town envied in their elegance by the critical old colonels who sit in corners and count the cads who have slipped past the committee.

Suddenly something terrifying happened. Perhaps Heywood saw a shadowy figure beside him, an old man who despite a lifetime of alcohol and cholesterol was as straight as an arrow and no wider, an old man who shook his head sympathetically and patronizingly at his son. Whatever the reason, Heywood went into his usual round-shouldered stance, grabbed up his rumpled, discarded suit, and began to empty its pockets of his survival kit—flask, wadded roll of money, flat fifty tin of cigarettes, six packs of matches, three handkerchiefs, and several thick memo pads with one phone number on each pad.

By the time he had stuffed the new suit with all this stuff, giving the coat several destructive wrenches in the process, he was the familiar ruined Broun again. He was in the useful

French phrase "Hors Concours," present but not asking for any prizes.

I wanted to say something encouraging about how he had looked for a few moments, but I was already old enough to know that when you catch people alone with their dreams, it's best to keep your mouth shut. I understood, however, why he had gone to so much effort to get his puttees on backward for the uniform inspection.

• •

In the years between the return from the war and the purchase of the house on Eighty-fifth Street, Heywood's career had prospered. War correspondent, dramatic critic, sports writer, he was obviously the kind of colorful columnist-personal diarist who was to be the phenomenon of the twenties and thirties, the sort of person who one day talked about the world and the next about a birthday necktie.

His column was at first called "Books and Things," but he was not very disciplined about his reading and wrote less and less about books and more about things. When his editor gave him tepid encouragement in this direction by remarking, "The 'things' pieces are better than your book pieces," he shifted over to the title he was to make famous, "It Seems to Me."

He and the others on the opposite editorial page of the *World,* like the Broadway gossip columnists of the tabloids and the whole new breed of byline guides to every phase of life, were in a tradition that runs from the Athenian orators (Pericles for the *Times* and *Herald Tribune,* Cleon for the *News* and *Mirror*) to television talk show hosts. The influence of most of them was spectacular but transitory, like the waves made by a spoon in a dishpan, and sometimes one doubted how closely they were scanned. An elevator man reported to a family friend that he never missed a word of the brilliant "It Seems to Me" columns by that wonderful writer Edward Brown.

While Heywood was achieving recognition if not compre-
hension, Ruth began inexplicably to fade into an odd-job journalist whose jobs were increasingly less interesting and important.

She adduced all the familiar feminist arguments as causes of
the problem, and I heard of many employers—although never
by name—who turned her down for jobs because, as Heywood's wife, she didn't need a job. I accepted this explanation
as one devised to comfort me, since I liked, in those guilt-
hungry times, to assume that the birth of her child and the
subsequent disruption of her life by the child's illnesses were
the real cause of her problems.

After all, many of her friends, some of them burdened with
children and households without any live-in help, were working busily, and few of them had the distinguished résumé that
writer-editor Ruth Hale could present.

Looking with more care at the chronology, as I eventually
did, it occurred to me that when I was only six months old
Ruth had hired Mattie, a beleaguered teenager who had preserved through hunger, illiteracy, and a short, wretched marriage, a sweet, resilient, and understanding nature. Mattie
learned quickly and within another six months could have
taken care of me lovingly and capably during whatever working hours professional demands imposed on Ruth. I didn't
become a sickly distraction until I was almost five, so all the
pat answers dissolve, and we are left with the kind of specula-
tion that tries to make a whole dinosaur out of two teeth and
a toenail.

There was certainly no lessening of Ruth's energies, or even,
for a while, in her involvement in causes that brought her to
public attention. Newspaper clippings and law journal entries
attest that she spent a good deal of time harrassing the State
Department in an effort to get a passport issued simply to Ruth
Hale with no degrading compromises like "Mrs. Heywood

Broun, otherwise known as Ruth Hale." Secretary of State Charles Evans Hughes personally denied her second request, explaining in his letter that a consular official would be "placed in a most embarrassing position" when called on for help by a man "traveling with a woman who does not use his family name and yet claims to be married to him."

There is a ring of elegant pomposity about this that suggests the old Prime Minister of Graustark admonishing Princess Yetive for a hoydenish prank, but Ruth and her friends put much hard work into the briefs that supported what is now accepted as an unquestionably rational position.

She had not withdrawn to any boudoir, and would have roundly cursed any of her friends who gave that name to one of her rooms, but she had ceased to compete with Heywood as she had done up to her marriage and for a short time thereafter.

She certainly didn't stop because she thought competition was unseemly. True, she had as many rules of conduct as Queen Victoria, as I had learned long before I even understood what conduct was, but they were not the same as the queen's and never had to do with what was unseemly. The person who had hissed poor James Weldon Johnson was not concerned with the unseemly, and seemed, in fact, to seek it out and relish it. During the first years after the war she did such unseemly things as joining with Doris Fleischmann and Jane Grant to found the Lucy Stone League. Fleischmann and Grant, despite being married to publicist Edward L. Bernays and editor Harold Ross, also pursued careers, and, at first, when the odd jobs were fairly frequent, Ruth appeared to be doing the same.

The slogan of the League was "My name is the symbol of my identity which must not be lost." Lucy Stone, the nineteenth-century fighter for women's rights, first spoke them, and they have a fair and forthright ring.

Symbols are important, of course, sometimes more important than the complications of reality, but in Ruth's case, despite the depth of her emotional commitment to the symbol of her name and the cause of which it was a part, there was, I think, always hissing at her back that "basket of snakes," the family in Rogersville.

"Do you know why I hate my mother so much?" Ruth once rather startlingly remarked to me. "Because we're so much alike." I was twelve or so at the time and the remark, which I didn't understand, came after one of Annie Riley Hale's displays of disagreeable intractability about vegetarianism, which she espoused, feminism, which she despised, or a new kind of economics, which only she and two or three other people understood. She was always trying to get me to read the books of one of these fellow illuminati. Ruth and her mother seemed to me antitheses, one of them an eccentric and embarrassing old bigot radiating malevolence to the music of a lot of jangling costume jewelry, and the other an elegant spokesman for a rational world that was on its way.

My grandmother was the simpler personality of the two. Groucho Marx used to sing a song that ended with the refrain, "Whatever it is, I'm against it," and this could have been Annie Riley Hale's anthem. Offhand I can think of only two areas where her approval was likely. Scottish Presbyterians with sound ideas on economics were okay and so were a few English and Germans, but her voice was constantly, stridently raised against Catholics, Jews, Latins of all nations, Nigras who did not know their place, feminists who did not know that their place was in the home, and persons of all races and faiths who ate white bread. Despite her belief that a woman's place was in the home, she was seldom to be found in the California cottage to which she had moved when her family moved out, preferring to campaign around the country in her crusades for sound money and an end to vaccination (Ruth had nearly died of one as a child), or to settle in with one of her children and try to manage their lives in an improving way.

Looking back I realize that I was too self-concerned to notice the heavy knapsack of old notions that was slowing Ruth's progress toward the new world, notions Annie Riley had packed for her little girl's trip to the confusing society of the north.

After all, that stuff I was getting about what gentlemen did or did not do, had another side that we never discussed. There were, of course, things that ladies did or did not do. On the surface Ruth was clear and direct in her rebellion. She was defiantly happy to be among the first women to smoke in theater lobbies; she used improper words, as they used to be called, with an elegant relish that robbed them of vulgarity if not their shock; and she was firm in the campaign to keep her own name.

Still she had seen her mother run the household in Rogersville in the traditional southern manner of authority disguised as deference. One reason my grandmother was so hostile to feminism, it always seemed to me, was that she wanted no changes in a system that permitted her, at least, to enjoy the fruits of tyranny without any of the criticism that sometimes embitter them.

Battling with Annie Riley was like a pillow fight where some of the pillows were full of razor blades, and Ruth, not herself above the use of an unauthorized stiletto, brooded after the bouts about the similarities of their methods—the fear she had expressed to me of their likenesses. I was still at the age where puritans and fanatics were always people on the other side, and I could not see that the unflagging insistence of the nasal old virago was a cruel caricature of the articulate, witty rigidities of the new woman.

When they were doing feminism, which was a good deal of the time, the old lady sometimes lapsed into awful displays of what she considered to be properly feminine behavior, an act involving a lot of sidling, simpering, and swinging of coral beads that rattled distractingly while she told unlikely stories of the gallantries of the Old South.

It was in these softer moments that she would insist that I call her "Danny," a corruption of Granny, of which, at an early age, I had apparently once been guilty. Children don't like being reminded of their recent difficulties with the language and I often responded sullenly to these requests. Unlike Ruth, however, I never made the mistake of entering into debate, and was usually seen safe behind the barrier of a book.

Observing the two of them I realized even then that Annie Riley had one great advantage over her daughter, an advantage that made her unbearable but invulnerable. She was sure, to the very core of her being, that every one of her nutty ideas was engraved in the indestructible metal of *absolute right.* Doubts did not disturb her sleep or her thoughts, which is probably why she lived such a long and healthy life.

As Annie Riley had run the life of her shadowy husband, Ruth began practicing with her not so shadowy brothers. I do not remember Uncle Shelton, dead so tragically early of a brain tumor, but I do remember that his mother and his sister spent a lot of time knocking on the character of his widow. Had she wanted to run him too?

I do remember Uncle Richard's constant and gentle remonstrances of "Now, Mother"—"Now, Ruth," as the two strong characters fought over him like millstones over a bag of grain. I remember how jaunty he became, at last the patriarch, moving into his eighties with the springy step of the victor through survival. Just before ninety, fading fast, he tried for several days to tune the voice that had been so endlessly promising. It rattled and croaked discouragingly, but the man who had been so diffident and deferential when young was determined now, and suddenly achieving a full baritone production, called out in one long resonant note the perfection of his art, and died in the fullness of that triumph.

• WHOSE LITTLE BOY ARE YOU? •

It is too simple to say that his mother, his sister, and his wives bullied him or lived through him. It is true, though, that while Ruth lived he seemed much more a part of our household than any of those he briefly set up on his own, and it is true that like his much more successful brother-in-law, Heywood, he was oddly malleable in many ways.

I remember a cartoon someone drew in the twenties showing a very large Ruth sitting commandingly on top of a house, holding a pair of fire tongs as a symbol of authority, while inside the house a very small Heywood sat at a typewriter toiling away. I suppose in a rough and ready way the picture defined the way things were, except that, of course, the person who pounds the typewriter gets the praise, the credit. Even an unobservant little boy couldn't help but see how much Ruth shaped Heywood's ideas, how powerfully she could wheel up the artillery of logic and facts until, deprived of every weapon save the sword of charm, Heywood would twinkle his way out of the argument. Still, her ideas soon turned up in his work.

Once he lost a good deal of money gambling in Florida and sent a telegraphic request for money to Ruth in New York. Along with the cash she sent a long, angry, and well-reasoned wire on the subject of financial fecklessness. She showed me his reply, a wire that said "Love, Heywood." I was suddenly jealous that this seemed to work better than all the elaborate excuses I put forward for my own misdeeds.

The gray eminence business was the method of her time and of her background and she did it well but obviously came to hate it. In order that the fiction of their separate lives could work, Ruth had to have an income, and one of the exasperating but efficient ways in which this was arrived at was by making Ruth a de facto judge of the Book of the Month Club. Heywood turned over to her the piles of books he received as an official member of the Club's board and she wrote reports when they were needed, weeded out the ephemera, picked the book he would vote for, told him why he was voting for it, and sent him off to the meeting. In the boardroom of the Club hangs Joe Hirsch's portrait of the five original judges, Henry Seidel Canby, Christopher Morley, Dorothy Canfield Fisher, William Allen White, and Heywood. Perhaps if Ruth were in that picture instead of just being the endorser of the Club's checks, she might have felt better, but the role she had chosen made that impossible. She had a better, more informed taste, I think, than any of them, and in 1917 had celebrity credentials to match any of them save perhaps the relentlessly picturesque Morley.

The fire tongs had, however, lifted Heywood to that position of eminence that made him an obvious choice for the Book of the Month Club's expert group, despite the fact that he shared with his son a taste for the rhinestone glitter of picturesquely bad books, without his son's guilty knowledge of how bad the books were.

If all this had happened in Rogersville, Ruth might have been quite happy, steering her husband to eminence and sharing the secrets of her success with these ladies she could trust, but she had left all that behind—or perhaps not quite all—and the tables covered with jigsaw pieces and ruled pads for diagramless crosswords had a heartbreaking resemblance to the petit point frames and needlework gear that traditionally dulled the knife edges of feminine frustration.

For her, as for Heywood, the goals were always clear. She could see her new world, transformed by militant feminism, as he saw his, transformed by economic revolution.

When I think of their childhood nicknames, "Little Sister" and "Lilacs," I realize how far it was from where they were to where they wanted to be. You have to honor their efforts when you realize what a stretch they were at to ignore the nineteenth-century codes that had been driven into them by parental hammers, all those, rules from the large ones involving *sin* and *salvation*, to small distinctions of social behavior proper to all occasions.

I think suddenly of a dinner party not long before Heywood's death where the guest of honor was ex-heavyweight champion Gene Tunney. Getting away from *his* background, Tunney had become a wine enthusiast and expert and arrived with a couple of dusty bottles, one a white wine of some tremendous distinction, and the other an ancient brandy.

Sitting at the head of the table, Heywood certainly didn't look like an arbiter elegantium, but rather like Nero Wolfe after a particularly messy orchid potting session. He had on a yellow silk pajama top over an ancient sweat shirt, and striped flannel tennis pants whose stripes were largely obscured by smears of paint. These blobs came from Heywood's practice of cleaning his brushes on his pants when he was engaged in his hobby of creating the inept yet charming pictures always known as early Brouns. The only thing elegant about him were his patent leather evening shoes and they had lost some of their elegance when they lost their laces.

He looked like a man who could use lectures on almost all the niceties of life. Tunney, full of his new learning, launched into an oenological ABC that was punctuated by the command that we were all to wash out our mouths with black coffee in order to clarify the palate. We were at last allowed to sip the wine, and had its virtues explained in technical terms that made me feel that I was taking part in a laboratory experiment.

Heywood remained silent through all this and through the subsequent serving of dessert, vanilla ice cream. While this melted, Tunney told us about the brandy and how we should hold the glasses in order to bring out the bouquet. In the middle of this, Heywood suddenly and shockingly picked up his snifter and dumped the golden liquid into the puddle of ice cream that he then began to stir into an alcoholic goop.

"Try it this way, Gene," he said in a strange voice. "It's awfully good."

There was a stunned silence. Nobody else had quite the nerve to pour the aristocracy's tranquilizer into the cold cornstarch and cream, but poor Tunney was deflated. There was something in the tone of his host that was so arrogant and sure that there was the sudden doubt about what he had learned. Did the real nobs have odd customs not to be found in books?

I had meanwhile recognized Heywood's voice as that used by his father when depressing the pretensions of some fellow who thought he knew as much about champagne as Heywood Cox Broun.

When Tunney had gone home, I made one of my rare open criticisms of Heywood and taxed him with cruelty. "The poor man may have gone on a bit too much about it," I said, "but he's trying very hard to be somebody new and you kicked the props away." In the same odd voice, Heywood said, "I could hardly be expected to take instruction on wine from a fighter." Heywood Cox Broun, like Hamlet's father, was occasionally invisibly influential.

•   •

When Heywood Broun, the wine merchant's son, and Ruth Hale, the extensively self-educated refugee from Tennessee, sat down at the first Algonquin Round Table luncheon in the summer of 1919, they were taking part in a practical joke on Alec Woollcott, the whole business having been organized by Murdock Pemberton in order to have in the printed program and the banner that hung over the table as many misspellings as possible of Alec's name.

One account of the occasion says that Ruth dominated the talk with an account of her Freudian analysis. If this is so, it is the only occasion on which it was discussed and I never later heard anything about it.

• W H O S E L I T T L E B O Y A R E Y O U ? •

Ruth seems to me to have been a very unlikely prospect for successful analysis. The opening of doors to the cellars and attics of memory requires the removal of locks you put there yourself, and I do not see the proud and stubborn Ruth Hale letting anyone much past the front porch, let alone into the sealed rooms. As a person who was pleased to think of herself as modern and free of the restrictive rules of Rogersville gentility, she would certainly feel that she must speak warmly of the new therapy, and it's my guess that at the luncheon somebody doubted that Freud was more than a fad and that Ruth rushed to the rescue. To demonstrate a belief one ends up eating the doubtful mushroom, drinking the long-opened wine, or offering to undergo a course of treatment.

The person who is successfully analyzed is supposed to have come to terms with the irrationalities of life and to have ceased self-torment about unavoidable imperfections—I know that's oversimplified but it's not that inaccurate—and Ruth Hale was not one to come to terms.

Cyrano de Bergerac, a textbook neurotic who denied reality at every turn, was proud, at his ridiculous and unnecessary death, that, whatever he had lost, he had retained his panache, his white plume.

Ruth understood the price of keeping one's panache and paid it. One part of this price is a generous amount of anger, and I suppose the energy used up by Ruth in the series of fights about things supremely important and supremely unimportant —panache wearers are often vague about which is which— may have been drawn from her treasury of creativity.

Certainly the end to which most of her creativity was finally put, the advancement of Heywood's career through criticizing his writing, correcting it, and sometimes simply doing it, may have been the right thing for Annie Riley's daughter to do, but it was hardly a happy end for the Ruth Hale who was fighting for identity through the Lucy Stone League.

Also when all the day's battles had been fought and Heywood's mind bent in some new and interesting direction, there seemed to be a number, a terrifying number, of hours left over, and Ruth's second-floor living room became increasingly cluttered with card tables bearing puzzles, piles of cigarette butts, and boxes of Requa's Charcoal Tablets, a stomachic whose presence seemed to prove that idleness can roil up the digestion as badly as does executive strain.

There was a stretch of several years when we were still at Eighty-fifth Street when a good deal of the extra time was soaked up by the mechanics of entertaining, Ruth planning menus while Mattie bustled about the primitive basement kitchen that produced its sophisticated dishes with the weary help of an ancient icebox and a woodburning stove.

Sitting in the Algonquin lobby at ninety, looking back at the table that floated in his faraway layer of memory, Marc Connelly tried to find me an umbrella phrase that would cover the stretch from the Mermaid Tavern aspect of the old bunch to its less worldly guise, Lady's Day at the Lodge.

"We all loved each other," Marc said at last. "We hated to be apart." "After lunch here we went to somebody's house and figured out some place to have dinner." Very often it was our house and Mattie improvised something with eggs.

Extensively they lived in each other's apartments and houses. When Ruth turned over the second house on her Stamford property to Murdock, there was no nonsense about rent. Deems Taylor lived in our house while he wrote an opera called *The King's Henchman;* Woollcott and Ross rancorously but extensively shared an apartment; Ross and Jane Grant rented my room while I was in Atlantic Highlands. Frank Sullivan, who sometimes needed several months to build up nerve to get back to his home in Saratoga, stayed with pretty nearly everybody during these stretches. The Algonks lent each other money, found doctors and psychiatrists for each other, and, best of all, listened to each other's troubles. At an early age I was run in as a kind of useful stooge on cheerup sessions. I cannot have been more than eight years old when Ruth said to me one night, "Deems Taylor is coming to dinner and he's very depressed, so I want you to ask him a lot of questions about his music, and after dinner ask him to play something for you."

I requested the "Looking Glass Suite" from the dream sequence of *Begger on Horseback,* the play Marc wrote with George Kaufman. It was the only piece of Deems' music that I knew, but he was pleased to be asked and played it.

I don't know that a single evening of being drawn out by a calculatingly wide-eyed small boy did anything for Deems, although he seemed in good shape when he left, and I don't know what he was depressed about. It was just one of many occasions when we, sometimes aided by our semi-permanent guest MacNamara, or by someone else who had been briefed, devoted ourselves to the simple therapy of attention.

Strings of people came up to Stamford, few to be treated as roughly as Mrs. Parker in the Case of the Giant Rats, some to bemoan writers' blocks, others, romantic blocks and all the private troubles that lay under the round dance of fun that these witty talented people were supposed to be enjoying.

At one point James Dunn, later a star in *A Tree Grows in Brooklyn,* but then a song and dance man, hid out in Stamford for over a month while being sought both by the police and the Mob, both anxious to have his recollections of a shooting at the Howdy Club. When the case was eventually solved, he said a thankful goodbye to a life not geared to a Broadway boy.

A father and son pair of English actors, Hugh and John Buckler, spent almost an entire summer with us because no one had the nerve to ask when they were leaving, and they hadn't the jobs that would have made departure desirable.

The closest they came to a demanded departure was when

young John Buckler, told to watch me as I swam in the grasp
of water wings, sloped off into the woods at the wrong moment. The moment happened to be that in which a neighboring
farmer's dog playfully bit a hole in my wings, which permitted
the air on which I depended to escape rapidly. To my own
surprise I swam unaided from the middle of the pond to the
dock. I then rushed home to announce that I was now able to
swim in grown-up fashion.

It was when I sank during the subsequent demonstration of
the new skill that the Bucklers were on the verge of packing,
but as always, hard hearts were reserved for ourselves, and our
useless decorative guests hung on until some company of *Dangerous Corner* took them out on the road.

At least they didn't shoot me as did a retired Australian Air
Force major who managed several months of room and board
as sort of caretaker in whichever house was empty. He didn't
mean any harm—"Who would guess an air pistol had such
power! I mean, just a spot of practice, what? Have to keep the
old eye keen in case one's called up." The bruise went away
about the same time he did.

If Dunn came because of legal troubles, Dorothy Parker
because of medical troubles, the Bucklers and the major because of financial troubles, many others arrived at the old
wooden house as they might have at some retreat or sanitar-
ium. If Ruth and Heywood had received psychiatrists' rates for
trouble-listening, the repairs to the house might quickly have
been paid for. Of course, a psychiatrist might fairly say that
their advice, obviously uninformed in any scientific way, was
only worth a few shingles, but undeterred, the troubled kept
turning up on the doorstep.

I wasn't then aware, of course, that Heywood and Ruth were
pretty close to the top of the list among the troubled. Perhaps
if we had lived in an apartment, I might have heard the anxious
voices through the walls, seen the tears before they were wiped

away, or been more aware of the tension that contiguity makes impossible to conceal.

•   •

In the loneliness-freedom and isolation-safety of the layered life on Eighty-fifth Street, however, I assumed that terror, like me, was confined to the third-floor front.

I don't remember when they began, but the fears that make breathing a real effort were, by the time I became a member of the downstairs therapeutic team, extensive and no less awful because most of them were silly.

The most common involved the discovery of some small sin or mistake of mine that had blossomed into a disaster. I once, for instance, dropped somebody's embroidered handkerchief in the toilet. The loss was not noticed or discovered, but I had weeks of cold sweating in the dark as I saw the whole plumbing system exploding from the clog, the discovery of the handkerchief plug, the tracing of its arrival there to me—stammering, unable to explain, and weighted with guilt suited to some complex and horrible four-ply mortal sin.

Nothing happened to the plumbing, but by the time I was sure of that I had some other one to worry through the night like a tooth, and to seize me unexpectedly in the daytime like the hand of unquestioned authority.

Some of them only worked at night like my fear of Dr. Fu Manchu. By day and even through the early evening I devoured the Doctor's improbable adventures as set down by Sax Rohmer and enjoyed them immensely. At night it occurred to me that the sinister mandarin might be angry with me for siding so openly with Commissioner Dennis Nayland Smith of the Burmese Constabulary in his defense of the Western world.

In such case it would be childishly easy for Fu to send one of his Dacoits, little men with silk strangling cords, to the roof of our house. Some complicated and cruel process, something to do with being kept on racks, had stunted their growth so they could hide anywhere. One would, in fact, fit inside the laundry hamper visible from my bed. My breath would grow shallow and rasping as I watched the lid of the basket. Would it slowly begin to rise? If so, what would I do? How I longed for the "service revolver" that every Englishman in the books I was reading seemed always to have handy.

On other occasions I watched the window in case the Dacoit chose to lower himself, as he often did in the books, by his deadly rope and come in over the top of the grating that was supposed to keep me from falling out of the window. In this case I listened for the peculiar whining cry characteristic of these terrible people that I assumed a confederate in the street would utter when there were no witnesses to report a powerful dwarf descending our wall.

By day, it always seemed to me that the Si Fan, the powerful group of which Fu Manchu was a member, didn't really give a damn what I thought, since I couldn't imagine that I was much of an obstacle to their plan for world domination, but the dark was another matter and I really didn't know what to whistle going past the graveyard where my self-confidence seemed to lie buried.

After a while I discovered a palliative for those problems, which was to establish a very small world under a quilt, a world that long after official bedtime contained a warm bright reading lamp and books about Tom Swift, Jerry Todd, The Rover Boys, and others whose problems while interesting did not involve themselves with the forces of evil, beyond occasional muckers who cheated at games and cursed when they lost.

When I was in my feathery tent the Dacoit could have gotten out of the laundry basket and tap-danced without my noticing, and the awful list of *things* caused by my unforgivable clumsiness, forgetfulness, laziness, and maliciousness stayed pretty much folded up. My only problem was to make sure of turning out the light before the power of sleep proved stronger than the narrative power of Tom Swift's creators, a group called Victor Appleton. Of course, the night finally came when it seemed so certain that Tom's electric airship was going to drop into the crater of a volcano or onto the polar icecap (the details grow hazy after a half century) that I kept on reading until Tom and I both fell unconscious, he under the weight of the collapsed gasbag and I under the even greater weight of exhaustion. The quilt then came to rest on the bare light bulb and shortly the smell of burning feathers brought a rescue party.

The satisfactory outcome of such a situation from a small boy's point of view is a lot of yelling and a few mildly stinging blows followed by the resumption of sleep, all guilts removed by the rough words and rough handling.

No such simple solution was available in a household where I was both a small boy and a miniature adult expected to be as rational as the full-scale model, and a disappointment when standards of reason and maturity were not met.

Before the light was extinguished for the second time, I was told that we would talk this over in the morning and decide what was to be done. The adrenalin of fear then sent exhaustion down the stairs with Ruth and Heywood and I lay awake running through all the awful variations on the trial scene we were so shortly to play.

It was just as bad as I feared. They asked whether they could come to my room and once in, filled it to overflowing with gentle sadness. They were genuinely sorry that I had proved unworthy of trust and they questioned me with the relentless persistence of a dentist fishing around in a root canal as to why I had betrayed this trust. I couldn't very well tell them about the menace of Fu's agents or about the general feeling I had that life was free of fears only when I was in my soft cell with a good book. They would laugh at the first idea and be hurt by the second one since they were under the impression that, out of the lessons of their own fear-ridden childhoods, they had set up a system under which I would be entirely free of anxiety.

I didn't take much part in the discussion, limiting my replies to "I'm sorry" and "I don't know" (to efforts at finding out why I had behaved so irresponsibly). I had to be careful not to shrug my shoulders at any point because shrugging was rude and rudeness was, in this desperately civilized house, *the ultimate sin.* One could be sarcastic, minatory, or even, along prepared tracks, inflammatory, but rudeness was a kind of stiletto to be used only in extremis.

Once Ruth taxed me after some dinner party with rudeness to a guest and I issued the standard "I'm sorry" and meant it since I liked the guest, didn't realize the nature of my transgression, and said so. Up went the single eyebrow that was the flash of lightning before the crack of thunder.

"May I remind you, Woodie, of the words of Oscar Wilde? A gentleman is never unintentionally rude."

Well, what do you say to that? My grubby, seven-year-old hands seemed to swell into big red balloons as I waved them weakly about and tried to find some way out. Regret wasn't enough, ignorance was no excuse, and the eyebrow stayed up all through my balloon dance.

The end of our discussion on the subject of the burned quilt was the selection of two punishments, one having to do with restrictions on my allowance and the other on my evening reading time. To show that no old-fashioned tyranny was involved here, I was allowed my choice between the two. I think I took the reading penalty and started using a flashlight in my tent, which was hard on the eyes but harmless to cloth when it fell out of hand during one of fun-loving Tom Rover's duller pranks.

My father, Heywood, likened his father to characters in Thackeray: "fashionable, far-off men."

Paul Thompson.

Grandmother Broun would have frightened Henry James, charmed Edith Wharton.

Cousin Helen Baker
was Talleyrand
disguised as a spinster
schoolteacher.

Aunt Vera Broun,
Uncle Irving's wife,
found us all
frightening.

Once long ago, for just a moment, Uncle Fritz Brosé had the world on a string.

Heywood was not yet called "Lilacs" when this picture was taken, but it is not the outfit most boys would choose for themselves.

Uncle Irving Broun, and his daughter Almeda, viewed Christmas a lot more merrily than I did.

Ruth's mother, Annie Riley Hale, in a rare moment of quiet draws a relieved smile from dutiful son Richard.

Cousin Kathryn Herbert survived, unscarred, my effort to club her senseless.

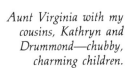

Aunt Virginia with my cousins, Kathryn and Drummond—chubby, charming children.

For a good friend, the photographer
Nick Muray, Ruth let a little of
her vulnerability show.

Despite appearances, I have never
learned to knit. I have enough
trouble tying my shoes.

Getting off by herself must have been a treat for factotum Mattie, who was unflappable but not inexhaustible.

Briefly, Ruth and I were ready for the cover of a comfy woman's magazine. We must both have been surprised when we looked at the picture later. In fact, I already look surprised.

Manning Harr

Chauffeur Earl Wilson is on the running board of the car in which he taught me to drive.

My neurotic frown was early-born.

This is the face with which Ruth
efied Charles Evans Hughes and
all the hosts who spoke of
compromise.

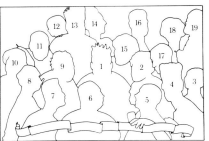

(1) Alexander Woollcott: Sometimes a dear friend to Ruth and Heywood, sometimes a spitting enemy. (2) Harpo Marx: As good a cardplayer as he was a musician. (3) Paul Hyde Bonner: Novelist and bon vivant. (4) George S. Kaufman: Playwright and mordant wit. (5) Raoul Fleischmann: Publisher of The New Yorker, but wise enough not to tell Harold Ross how to run it. (6) Socialite Gerald Brooks: A school classmate of Heywood's. (7) Henry Wise Miller: A banker who must have been more than a banker to get into this game. (8) Franklin P. Adams: He ran the "Conning Tower" column in The World, and was best man at Ruth and Heywood's wedding. (9) Heywood. (10) Dorothy Parker: She was thinking up things to say at the following day's lunch. (11) Robert Benchley: He was soon to leave the certain miseries of a writer's life for the uncertain miseries of an actor's. (12) Irving Berlin: It would be presumptuous to identify him further. (13) Harold Ross: Editor of The New Yorker and among the wisest men of his time. (14) Beatrice Kaufman A better card player than her husband, and a woman who forgave Alec Woollcott more insults

than deserved forgiving. *(15) Alice Duer Miller:* *She's remembered for* The White Cliffs of Dover, *and wife to banker Henry. (16) Herbert Bayard Swope: Boss on* The World *of the players and later host to the game. (17) George Backer: Then a reporter, later publisher of the* New York Post. *(18) Joyce Barbour: An English actress attractive enough to be allowed to watch an all-American poker game. (19) Crosby Gaige: Theatrical producer.* Pastel by Will Cotton, 1929, from a private collection.

The unmade bed in an unmade bed
by Al Hirschfeld.

F.P.A. shared space with Heywood on the Op-Ed page of The World. *Frank is now about to share Heywood's money.*

Russell Aikens

This is the Congress of Vienna as Westbrook Pegler, Heywood, and Quentin Reynolds, who was later to sue Peg, unite in concentration on the seventh card. The kibitzer is my school friend Al Horton.

HEYWOOD BROUN
for Congress

The political predilections of artists can push noses into odd poses, 1930 and 1938.

TRUTH

Will you help Broun carry this Torch to Wash.?

[This is a drawing of Heywood Broun, Socialist candidate for Congress from the 17th district, Manhattan, made by Percy Crosby, the famous creator of "Skippy," as his contribution to the Broun campaign.]

Percy Crosby, who drew the Skippy comic strip, did his best to send Heywood to Congress but, as usual, art was outpointed by mammon.

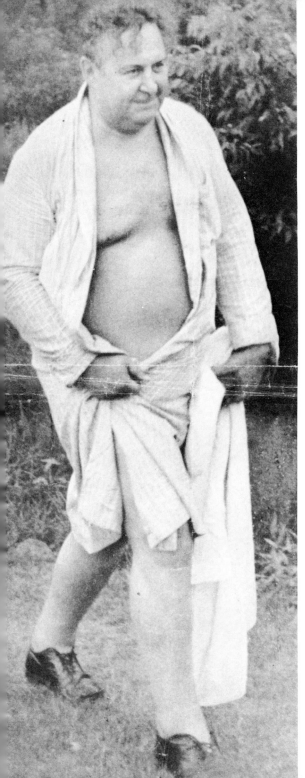

*Heywood managed to be
sloppy even in a bathrobe.
The shoes were not up to his
usual standards.*

Frank Adams had a reputation as a grouch, but I liked him because he came early to our parties so he could play store with me. *Courtesy, the Hampden-Booth Theatre Library at The Players, New York.*

Paul's smile rose like the sun and, for me, lit up the hours I spent with him. *Courtesy, S. Schaefler.*

Mac looked so much like an Irish policeman that it was hard to believe he had been one, easy to believe that he always played one. *Courtesy the Hampden-Booth Theatre Library at The Players, New York.*

Connie, my stepmother, was Heywood's designated runner in the charity softball games organized by Lowell Thomas.

At the Arizona Desert School, I am astride the headmaster, 1932.

Since I was convalescing from nephritis at this time, it took an Olympic effort to get over the big frog, 1935.
Courtesy, UPI.

Heywood and Connie toasting on a Caribbean island.

Connie's daughter, Pat, got a quick introduction to the publicity world and an autograph from Fred MacMurray.

As a college sophomore, I helped, in my attention-getting vest, to direct the school musical starring the soon-to-be-psychiatrist Nathan Kline, on whose shoulder I have a guiding hand. He played Groucho Marx and I followed, distantly, in the footsteps of Elmo Lincoln as Tarzan, 1938.

Karl E. Fortess

Myself and son, who was later to be, as novelist Hob Broun, the fourth generation of professional writers in our family. The first wa[s] Annie Riley Hale with an intemperate attack o[n] Theodore Roosevelt.

After playing an old married couple in Putnam, Connecticut, in 1949, Jane Lloyd-Jones and I shortly became a young married couple in real life. We lost our daughter at the right at the end of the run.

Leo Durocher, newly made manager of the New York Giants, was happy to see a friendly face from Ebbets Field.

Mark Connelly is in full cry, thus explaining my rapt expression and that of actress Jane Lloyd-Jones, my wife, 1965.

A half century in the saddle.

At the Arizona Desert School for Boys, Tucson, 1931.

Cotopaxi, Colorado, 1975.

• WHOSE LITTLE BOY ARE YOU? •

My more attractive behavior was the subject of many of Heywood's columns in the early twenties, and a bunch of his observations on how to rear children, or at least his child, were collected under the title "H. 3d, a Review of a Continuous Performance," which was then included in a collection called *Seeing Things at Night,* a book dedicated to Heywood Broun 3d.

In later years I used to get angry when reading over these pieces that seemed to make me into a comic little booby whose insufficiencies were paraded for the amusement of the reader and whose difficulties with a sensible perception of the world in which he lived were the beginnings of self-satisfied little sermons. I don't know whether the years make you any smarter but, if you're lucky, they make you forgiving, and I wonder now why I never saw the insecurity behind all that relentless jauntiness.

In December of 1919 when I was well into my second year, Heywood came across a book called *Were You Ever a Child?* by the then popular novelist Floyd Dell, who had become an expert on child psychology by that method that makes any American an expert, the putting of one's opinions, however baseless, between hard covers.

Commenting on Dell's book, Heywood got into a specula-tion that ran through several days in his column and which is a wonderful example of Heywood at the typewriter, easy, urbane, laughing at his worries, and very different from the man who could worry himself into heart palpitations when the dark force inside him woke up and began twisting his nerves.

"The only trouble with all the new theories about bringing up children," wrote Heywood, "is that it leaves the job just as hard as ever."

We believe in the new theories for all that. They work we think but, like most worthwhile things, they are not al-ways easy. For instance H. 3d came into the parlour the other day carrying the carving knife. Twenty years ago I could have taken it away and spanked him, but then along came the child psychologists with their talk of breaking the child's will, and sensible people stopped spanking. Ten years ago I could have said, "Put down that carving knife or you'll make God feel very badly. In fact, you'll make dada feel very badly. You'll make dada cry if you don't obey him." But then the psychoanalysts appeared and pointed out that there was danger in that. In trying to punish the child by making him feel that his evil acts directly caused suffering to the parent there was an unavoidable tendency to make the child identify himself with the parent subconsciously. That might lead to all sorts of ructions later on. The child might identify himself so completely with the father that in later life he would use his shirts and neckties as if they were his own.

Of course, I might have gone over to H. 3d and, after a short struggle, have taken the carving knife away from him by main force but that would have made him mad. He would at length have suppressed his anger and right away a complex would begin in his little square head.

Picture him now at thirty—he has neuralgia. Somebody mentions the theory of blind abscesses and he has all his teeth pulled out. No good comes of it. He goes to a psychoanalyst and the doctor begins to ask questions. He asks a great many over a long period of time. Eventually he gets a clue. He finds that when H. 3d was eight years old, he dreamed three nights in succession of stepping on a June bug.

"Was it a large, rather fat June bug?" asks the doctor carelessly as if the answer was not important.

"Yes," says H. 3d, "it was."

"That June bug," says the doctor, "was a symbol of your father. When you were three years old he took a

carving knife away from you and you have had a suppressed anger at him ever since. Now that you know all
about it your neuralgia will disappear."

And the neuralgia would go at that. But by that time
I'd be gone and nothing could be done about this suppressed feud of so many years' standing. My mind went
through all these possibilities and I decided it would be
simpler and safer to let H. 3d keep the carving knife as
long as he attempted nothing aggressive. A wound is not
so dangerous as a complex.

"And anyhow," I thought, "if he can make that carving
knife cut anything, he's the best swordsman in the flat!"

Three days later Floyd Dell weighed in with a letter that
appeared in the column, saying in part:

Psychoanalytically speaking I think you were wrong
about H. 3d and the carving knife. There is really no
Freudian reason why, when he came into the parlour, you
should not have gone over to him and, "after a short
struggle," have taken it away from him by main force. Of
course, that would have made him mad. But what harm
could that have done?

Unless, of course, you had previously represented
yourself to him as a Divine and Perfect Being. In that case
this new conception of you as a big bully would have had
to struggle with his other carefully implanted and nourished emotions—and his sense of the justice of your behavior might have been "repressed."

A couple of days later a Washington neurologist wrote to say
that since curiosity and imitation were encouraged among children, it was useless to say "Don't" to them every time they
showed active curiosity or attempted imitation. As to Dell's

notion that parents should not represent themselves as *perfect*, Dr. Reed said briskly, "The deification of the parent occurs in accord with the ancestor worship of primitive forebears, and the father will remain the god to the child as long as observation daily reveals the parent a worker of miracles."

The business of the carving knife and several other extensively reported episodes in the amusing childhood of H. 3d give a picture of a relaxed father who is ready to listen to anyone—even occasionally H. 3rd—in his search for correct parental posture. A shadowy figure called "Miss X" or occasionally simply "R" had a much smaller part in the reported handling of the child than Ruth actually played, but I don't think she much wanted to be part of this fantasy that flowed fifty-fifty from A. A. Milne and Sigmund Freud.

In fact, they were fearful about the whole family adventure from the beginning. As I heard it, the idea was Heywood's in the first place and it was he who expressed the yearning not so much for a child as for *a son*. This, I suppose, was to prove that although he could not shoot a gun, or hit a billiard ball, or dazzle the ladies as that Monsieur Beaucaire of Brooklyn Heights, his father, he could, by helping to produce a man, prove that in the basic sense he was one.

Ruth had told her brother Richard a few months before her wedding that she would never marry, and shortly after that she told him that she was certainly never going to have any children. Whether the change of heart in this case was out of some wish to make Heywood happy or out of some wish of her own, too deep to be found, was never a subject of discussion, although she used to tell me that she was glad I was a boy because it gave Heywood what he wanted in the only chance he was going to have to get it. He was much more the "Where-are-your-rubbers-do-you-have-your-muffler" parent than she, the worrier when I got home later than expected, the checker of my temperature even when I had no complaints.

This was perhaps not surprising in a man who carried about his own cardiograms for display to friends, a habit that once led Woollcott to the waspish suggestion that he hold a one-man show of them.

One precious gift they had for me was supposed to be as all powerful as those blessings that fairy princesses drop into the cradles of the fortunate. By making certain that I had no religious education of any kind, they were going to spare me from terror. They were convinced that their own lives were shadowed beyond saving by the vigorous nineteenth-century Christianity that they had rejected but had not, in the darkness of their dreams and fears, escaped. There was some puzzlement when I announced to them that thunderclaps were "God showing his ankle," and the subsequent discovery that this was my misinterpretation of a nursemaid's statement that it was "God's anger," led, I believe, to the dismissal of the nursemaid.

I did not confide in them my fear that God possibly spoke some language other than English, a circumstance that would make it impossible for me to convey a number of things urgently needing attention, but I did reduce them to actual gasping anxiety with the announcement, when I was about ten, that since a number of my school friends were attending the nearby Universalist Sunday School, I thought I might give it a try myself.

The Universalist Church, now merged into the Unitarian, was hardly a hellfire camp-meeting organization, but Ruth and Heywood treated the news like people seeing the first birdshot pustules of smallpox on smooth skin.

They summoned Dr. Alvan Barach, Heywood's sometime psychiatrist, on a house call whose purpose was not so much to dissuade me as to comfort them and convince them that this terrifying symptom might be no more than a sign of some juvenile emotional rash. I don't know how he handled the matter, although many, many years later he told me that their anxiety had been deep and genuine, but after a year of collecting attendance stars and Biblical paragraphs I drifted away from what seemed to me a friendly headmaster God, unlikely to do much more for me than the usual "Wait 'til you're a little older," which is such a staple among fair-minded headmasters.

I have often told the story of this psychiatric consultation as a piece of rueful comedy, but, however silly its surface, it is a wonderfully touching proof of parental devotion, and I didn't figure out that part of the story until much later. As far as I am concerned, shyness should be included high in any revised list of the Seven Deadly Sins, because looking unprofitably back I see example after example of spectacular affection that went for nothing because of the chilly cloaks in which they were disguised.

Consider, for instance, an occasion during my first year of boarding school, when, at age eleven, I took part in a medieval pageant that filled an otherwise charming spring day with the endless and boring rattle of children's voices singsonging through insipid lines of their own writing while they moved stiffly around in unconvincing costumes of their own making. It must have seemed to the few spectators, a group that included Ruth and Heywood, as long as the Hundred Years War and as inconclusive. If, after the drive up to Croton-on-Hudson and a long day standing around watching a school play, they had said something simple like "You were very good," their virtue would have been rewarded by happiness shared. As it was, being shy and having been, as I much later discovered, suffocatingly proud of my efforts (I did, after all, have three major roles), they did what the shy do on such occasions and hid their feelings behind a couple of little jokes. I thanked them stiffly and wished that like most of the other parents, they hadn't come.

I suppose it is possible that the whole of the *little adult* business under which I staggered through those early years might be explained as the shy parents' way of dealing with a child who might otherwise be given to giggling, crying, and displaying the barbaric behavior that invites those not shy to join in the giggling, pet the sobber, or on occasion engage in the intimacy of shouting at the barbarian or dealing out a couple of emotional, educational wallops.

Later when I became a vain little performer of songs at parties, I judged approval to be more professional than affectionate, a good notice, an impersonal encouragement.

In popular fiction shyness is a stimulus. The heroine says something shyly and the hero, inflamed, declares the love he has been concealing because of a feeling of his own unworthiness. Roused, he at last dares to aspire to this wonderful person whose very shyness is a proof of her purity and delicacy. His passion overcomes her shyness and happiness ensues. What does one do when all parties are shy?—nothing useful.

In fact, of course, shyness is just the inability to be open and spontaneous and is frequently merely a nice word for cold.

On our dining table in Eighty-fifth Street was a silver dinner bell inscribed in the eerily correct script that engravers use, "To Darling Grandpapa from Ethel, Alma and James." You may ask why I remember this piece of trivia when I cannot remember some of the addresses to which we moved from that house, and the answer is simple.

Ruth and Heywood were always talking and joking about the bell and its soppy message. What sort of people, ran the humorous speculations, would actually refer to a relative as "Darling Grandpapa." Ethel, Alma, and James were pictured as silly sentimentalists who worked locks of hair into remembrance rings and wrote gushy poetry on birthday cards.

They were part of the world from which Ruth and Heywood had escaped. "Darling Grandpapa," indeed! In a house where as equals we addressed each other by our first names, each

ringing of that bell (summoning Mattie who continued to address her employers as Miss Hale and Mr. Broun although
urged not to be so formal) was a declaration that we had moved
on into the age where emotion had better uses than the personal.

At first I felt that Ethel, Alma, and James were really rather
nice. I thought that I would enjoy a gift that publicly proclaimed my darlingness, but I soon learned that emotion was
for big things like *causes*. My counterfeit emotion as I pounded
the face of Warren Harding and called for the election of Debs
was okay, but a column of Heywood about my crying as a baby
got all mixed up with some whimsy as to whether I was really
crying because of the suspension of the Socialist assemblymen
in New York or the suppression by censors of James Branch
Cabell's *Jurgen*. "And after I thought of those things it seemed
to me that he was entirely justified in crying," wrote Heywood,
"and that I ought to be ashamed of myself because I didn't cry,
too, since there were so many wrong things in the world to be
righted."

Certainly it occurs to me now as it was always occurring to
me then that they were doing a good deal to right the world's
wrongs and that grumblings are unworthy, but I wish I had
known how much of this pose of theirs was thought and not
felt how much they wanted me to give them a dinner bell.

I had a hint in my teens when I went to the 1933 Chicago
World's Fair and brought back a couple of ashtrays on which
names could be baked. I had one for each of them. I had drawn
a rather crude fat man on Heywood's but nothing on Ruth's,
because, I think, I was a little afraid to try my dreadful sketch-
ing powers on breasts. Feelings were hurt because her gift was
impersonal, and I realize now that a "To Darling Mama" inscription might have caused a lot of scornful laughter and
secret pleasure. At the time I sighed and wondered at my
tendencies to wanton wounding.

• WHOSE LITTLE BOY ARE YOU? •

If the ashtray business revealed something of Ruth's true feelings, Heywood's came blazing out when he returned a couple of years later from a visit to Art Young, the great *New Masses* cartoonist who was dying in a nursing home.

"Do you know what's wrong with the radical movement?" cried Heywood. "There's no feeling. You're either useful to the cause or as good as dead. Do you know that not a single person has been to see him in months?"

I was smart enough not to say that I thought emotions were to be saved for causes, but not smart enough to embrace him.

In disciplinary matters Ruth was less inclined than Heywood to go along with the flexible precepts of the Association for the Advancement of Progressive Education, a group that had the ear of almost every New York intellectual parent. Not only did she set the stern Oscar Wildean standards about rudeness, she also saddled me with another adult concept that I am sure would not have gone down well in the relentlessly understanding world of progressive education.

I was only eight when the iron collar of honor was clamped around my neck, and its galling weight aroused an anger the extent of which I was not to know until long after both of them were gone.

It had become my custom, after a confusing day at the most progressive school then existing in the whole country, to soothe myself with the certainties of *good guys* against *bad guys* at a local silent movie house that provided two features changed daily.

Unhappily, the theater did not cater just to sensible people like me, who were interested in the active defeat of evil, but also to a bunch that feasted on love pictures, endless shots of kissing, crying, then kissing again.

Since I had to persuade an adult to take my money, pretend that we were related, and escort me inside, there were often exasperating delays during which some part of the adventure picture had passed before I could get in, which meant that I had to sit through the whole subsequent romantic blah before I could catch up.

For some weeks I had been looking forward to the arrival at the theater of the great silent star Elmo Lincoln in a Tarzan film and I had, in preparation, read the entire existing multivolume life of Lord Greystoke, whose "thin veneer of civilization" Lincoln would be constantly casting off in this great film.

When the day came I told Ruth rather casually that I might be a bit late coming home from school, and explained the problems of having to sit through a certain amount of junk (films probably now enshrined in the Museum of Modern Art archives) in order to be sure of seeing all of Tarzan's adventures.

To my horror, Ruth, with equal casualness, replied that in any case I must be home by 6:30 because we were having a dinner party. Perhaps, she said, I could see the picture some other day. I explained the impossibility of this, pleaded that my presence or absence at the dinner party was unimportant, and that the guests should be pleased at not having to sit next to a little kid perched on a telephone book.

None of this worked. The generation that had been banished to the nursery or an early meal in the kitchen was redressing this wrong by seeing to it that its children were allowed to partake fully in family life, a new tyranny dressed in the red, white, and blue coat of freedom.

At last I played my ace, pointing out that this was not just a movie but my first-ever film about TARZAN, an event of an importance transcending any party anywhere. If this didn't work, I thought, I would simply disobey and accept whatever punishment I got to pick from among the bunch that would be offered for my consideration.

"You will be home by six-thirty," said Ruth. "I'm putting you on your honor." Now, of course, I could not disobey.

• WHOSE LITTLE BOY ARE YOU? •

Even now as I tell the story and try to laugh, I remember the terrible moment when, even as Lincoln wrestled with a lion, I realized from a last desperate check with the illuminated clock on the wall that I had to go. I was more prompt to arrive at 333 West Eighty-fifth Street than were the guests, but was I not, in the sad fiction we were maintaining, a co-host? So I sat between a couple of people who had wished for a less limited conversation than asking what I had done at school that day. I did not even sulk, since honor forbids sulking, but rage ran through my head as fierce as Lincoln's lion but with no one to attack. You cannot attack honor. My anger at Ruth was so great that it had to be buried so deeply that I didn't really know it was there.

So, as the radical Heywood Broun was snooty to Gene Tunney on the occasion of the wine snobbery, the liberated Ruth Hale who had fled all the hollow formalities of Rogersville's social order had, after all, unknowingly brought them with her.

I suppose that Elmo Lincoln, the William S. Hart of the hunting knife, eventually plunged his blade between the ribs of Numa, the lion, and stood astride the corpse to give his triple yodel victory cry, a sound that would have been thrillingly rendered on the theater piano, but I'll never really know.

Years later influential friends offered to try to arrange a showing of the film in a MOMA screening room, assuming that the picture is in the files there, but no one could meet my first requirement for this event, that I be eight years old again and fascinated about a man raised by apes and permitted to behave like them anytime he pleased.

At the progressive school, whose name I shall conceal because it still exists and I'm sure is a much better place, we were permitted to behave in any way we wanted. About the only rule was that we had to call the teachers by their first names in the same kind of pretense at equality I had been dealing with at home.

Permitting a lot of children in the five- to ten-year-old range to express themselves creates a kind of kaleidoscopic behavior within the flashing facets of which much can happen that is ugly and frightening.

In the course of unstructured play on the roof, bullies established small reigns of terror, and the victims were warned that complaints to Hazel or Nadja would not only bring such unsatisfactory answers as "Work it out among yourselves," but would lead to terrible reprisals.

Recently the school unwisely wrote to me in a quest for funds, and just looking at the name on the envelope made me smell library paste and fear, the cloying scent of the atmosphere in which we created our poster-paint construction-paper art, and the sharp animal smell evoked by the poke, the pinch, and the whisper of scornful warning of what was going to happen to us on the roof.

The stilted formal manner I had acquired in my role as co-host of Eighty-fifth Street dinner parties, coupled with my small size, made me a perfect victim for not only full-scale bullies but also their toadies who were working their way, through sporadic practice, toward full-scale nastiness.

It was after a couple of these had worked me over between the swings and the seesaw that the chief tormentor approached with the idea of pulling my hair, bending my fingers, or doing any of the other things that amuse unsupervised children. Smarting from the first round of humiliation and fearful of the new torment, I suddenly felt my terror shift gears and become rage. I launched myself at the approaching ugly smile like a bony rocket. I landed a little low, my head hitting his stomach, but it was enough to overset him and in a moment I had the joy of grasping his ears and hammering his head on the floor. A few more good thumps, I thought, and he would be dead; I would be free of fear; and the roof would become a happy place on which to play.

I never achieved those triumphant bumps, however, because Nadja or Hazel or somebody got hold of my collar and dragged me off.

I sobbed in frustration as I complained that we were supposed to do whatever we wanted and what I wanted was to kill this beast who, under the blind eye of authority, had made us sick in anticipation of his ingenious meanness and sore as a result of his physical strength.

I suppose the school couldn't really permit manslaughter as just another form of creative play, but I don't know why it permitted this sandbox sadism either.

What I had learned at home, however, was learned again at school. Freedom was a cheat's word for responsibility. I was free only to do the right thing and rightness was not to be defined by me.

Things got better on the roof after my berserk moment but they didn't improve much downstairs, where the star pupils were those who excelled in making clay rabbits, watercolor genre paintings, and at following the music teacher in "Marching Through Georgia" on tom-toms and sandpaper blocks.

I was good at none of these things and at last, at my second progressive school, after making a copper box for Ruth, a box that couldn't be opened, a hollow brick too light to be a doorstop, I was banished to a makeshift class where with the dogged repetitiveness of a sweatshop worker, I hammered out fire irons. This second school was the first of the three boarding schools that finished up my precollege education and its principal virtue was that I got to come home on weekends, since it was only about forty minutes away from the city.

Like its predecessor, it was an uneasy mixture of frighteningly bright children and highly intellectual teachers with the serious flaw of very limited experience in day-to-day dealings with the young. Practical considerations were scamped. The school nurse, a friend of a friend of someone, was always cracking our spines with half-learned chiropractic technique, and a child unwary enough to complain of any internal distress had to drink warm water and bring it back up, presumably carrying off the poison that had caused the trouble.

We soon took to keeping our ailments to ourselves, although a few hacking gasps in class earned me a two-week quarantine for whooping cough, which I turned out not to have when somebody finally summoned a doctor.

The food was fashionably faddish and a breakfast of cracked wheat and apples was our inadequate preparation for a long walk from the dormitory to the classroom, a hike that took us across a golf course often covered in deep snow. On such occasions smaller children sometimes disappeared into sand traps from which they had as much difficulty in escaping as the duffers who used the place in the summer.

I don't know why I left it after only a year, but I was sorry to say goodbye to an interesting set of classmates and glad to say goodbye to luncheon sandwiches made from vegetarian bouillon paste.

It was, with its heavy emphasis on the arts, at all of which I was a hopeless underachiever, just the wrong place for wordy Woodie, and except for the brief triumph in the school's medieval pageant, I brought away no memories except of my own general scholastic inferiority.

When finally I arrived at an educational institution that approved of my sprawling but extensive book learning, the seeds of self-doubt were so well established in the cracks of my ego that weeding has filled many weary years.

In my fastness, education for me really took place on the third floor, the place where I did not have to be responsible, grown-up, or honorable.

From my bed I could see the reassuring HBIII monogram Ruth had worked into a blue circle on the end of my big white bookcase, half devoted to the books I intended to keep all my life like *Treasure Island, The Lost World,* and the ever-increasing chronicles of the doings of my enemy Dr. Fu, and half to a constantly shifting collection of juvenile junk and highly unsuitable review books quarried from the mounds of them that were to be found all over the first and second floors. I read a good deal of H. G. Wells' heavy and indigestible *History of the World* just because it was by the author of *The History of Mr. Polly,* with its picture of the joys of irresponsibility, and, despite a certain amount of confusing adult philosophy, its suggestion to me that things were going to get better when I got old.

I read with the wondering pleasure of a primitive examining the works of a clock. Much of what passed under my eyes was as mysterious as a set of cogs turning first one way and then the other, but the complexity of the whole business suggested that somewhere a great discovery was going to be made by those who persisted through enough books to discover the why of the cogwheel dance.

Science came to me through the *Book of Knowledge.* This vast work—there were, I believe, more than twenty volumes—was a sort of children's encyclopedia designed to make the complications of the new technology clear to the literal minds of the young to whom such concepts as the roundness of the world or the power of steam were not always believable, or in my case, interesting. The books were filled with homely examples that were designed to bring wonders down to some graspable level. So, I could tell you how many days it would take a train to reach the moon or any of the planets except the undiscovered Pluto. The tracks stretched poetically across the night sky in the *Book's* illustrations, and it didn't then occur to me that the train, as a symbol of speedy travel, was soon to be as laughable as the belief that the moon to which it was speeding was made of green cheese.

I learned that there was enough atomic energy in a glass of

water to lift the Woolworth Building six inches, although the secret of how to achieve this lift still lay hidden in the little pool of liquid.

I learned why the mercury rose in my thermometer, why the sky was blue, and the speeds of sound and light—which at least explained why distant cymbals came together well before we heard the clangorous results of their meeting.

I also discovered that buried in all the boring stuff about how the world worked there was in each volume a short section called the "Book of Golden Deeds." In these pages were recorded bits of richly gilded history of a noble sort. I learned about Mucius Scaevela who burned off his right hand in a fire to show his contempt for Lars Persona's tortures, and about Cincinnatus who left a plow in mid-furrow to save Rome. (I was a little puzzled that anyone should get credit for leaving a dull job driving a horse for an exciting job riding one, a job to be done with sword, armor, and banners.) I learned how an ancestor of Ruth's, Kate Douglas, saved the life of King James I of Scotland by sticking her arm where a door bar should have been while the king hid from his would-be assassins. Only much later did I learn that after smashing up Miss Douglas' arm they caught and killed the king anyway, and that later, caught by other Douglases, the murderers were crowned with red hot iron crowns. The "Book of Golden Deeds" didn't go in for these darker sides to its stories, and I read the little dramas with a lot more relish than I brought to my extensive and now totally out-of-date scientific education.

When I wasn't filling my head with facts, I was blowing it in odd directions with scented breezes of fantasy. To this end I spent long night hours standing on the windowsill of my bedroom leaning against what was to me a shoulder-high grating that was to protect me from accidental falls. From here I could watch for Dr. Fu Manchu's agents but I could also speculate romantically, luridly, or improbably about the people walking, talking, and driving in the street below, few of whom lived lives as interesting as those I planned for them.

After a while, of course, a nervous neighbor called to report the presence of a small boy on a precarious perch, and I was forbidden my crow's nest recreation.

In this case the admonition was soft and unaccompanied by any sort of punishment, although at the thought of Woodie held back from death by nothing but a wire grille attached to crumbling brownstone, they must have been sick with fear.

It seems odd that in the midst of grappling with their own extensive fears they worked so hard at trying to give me the easy passage they had missed—and that they were so bad at it. Of course, I never consciously thought of them as afraid of anything, although I knew that Heywood was a little nervous in automobiles. I knew this because he sat in the backseat singing pretty steadily through a series of college and drinking songs, punctuating the music with admonitions to whomever was driving to go slower. I didn't, however, realize that what I thought of as a little nervousness was occasionally a terror that made his ability to keep singing both admirable and amazing.

As befitted a son of Henrietta Brosé Broun, whose mother was a Sterling of Haverhill, Massachusetts, Heywood was very finicky in his language, and when occasionally taunted by Ruth over his inability to use four-letter words, would turn all red and shuffly before muttering the short sharp word at issue.

It surprised me, therefore, that so many of the songs from the backseat were what used to be called "dirty." Indeed, the one about what would happen to any Eli son of a bitch who invaded Harvard's halls is scarcely printable now. I suppose that as he visualized the terrifying series of accidents that waited around every corner, he decided that a gesture of daring and defiance was called for as a bracer to his courage, and what could be more daring than bellowing out the foul and forbidden.

When purged of defiance, he would turn to melancholy, and I often joined him in his favorite, a Crimean War dirge to be sung by a dwindling circle of officers. It went:

> *The mist on the glass is congealing,*
> *'Tis the hurricane's icy breath,*
> *And it shows how the warmth of friendship,*
> *Grows cold in the clasp of death.*
>
> *(Sturdily)*
> *Stand, stand to your glasses steady,*
> *And drink to your comrade's eyes,*
> *Here's a toast to the dead already,*
> *And a cup to the next man that dies.*

There was another equally gloomy verse that pointed out that "All the brightest have gone before us, and the dullest are left behind," and when we had finished that, Heywood, wishing to remain, however dull, among the living, would go back to badgering the driver, checking the speedometer, and calling for a law that would put governors on all cars.

During the singing sessions and other times when fears came close to the surface, I was at a loss to understand how grown-ups could be afraid, because it seemed to me that at the basic level they controlled their own lives. They were never sent to boarding school or to the MacKnights. If they became ill, they weren't punished with any cross-country trips, and even Heywood, fidgeting in the car he couldn't drive, told it where to go, which quite often was to take me to some railroad station.

Sudden, disrupting, involuntary departures aside, there was the question of government in the layered little kingdoms of Eighty-fifth Street. Ruth's and Heywood's floors were the domains of dictators who could keep the lights on as late as they liked, and who were able to summon subjects or, with equal ease, banish them, and could from time to time depart for destinations of their choice without any limits concerning the length of their absences.

My floor seemed no more than an Indian reservation, a place that was sort of mine but was also a place from which the authorities might send me away if they needed it or found me troublesome in my stubborn primitivity, and a place where *commissioners of criticism* were always visiting.

Ruth and Heywood never seemed to realize how much they confused me with all of their efforts at equality. The rigid, rule-filled households that had shadowed their early years were, in the case of their fortunate son, to be replaced with a kind of social democracy in which the sunshine of reason lit every corner and where discipline would lose its sting by being explained.

When I was three and had not yet been pushed into the achingly bright sunlight of rationality, I was apparently treated pretty much as other children were, that is, physically controlled when it was for my own obvious good and ordered about briskly and without amplifications as to why. I readily dealt with these circumstances by inventing a friend called Judge Krink, a jurist of unspecified jurisdiction but immense power who, as a matter of principle, never washed his hands. He went to bed when he chose and spent a good deal of his time playing in dirt. (He sounds, in fact, like a good many real-life judges.) Armed with his friendship, I did what I was told to, pointing out occasionally how silly the judge thought these orders to be. The device provided me with an outlet for frustration and provided Heywood with a whimsical column.

At its conclusion Heywood signaled, I now realize, the beginning of my premature journey into sort-of adulthood.

"When we asked about the Judge today there was no re-

sponse at first and it was only after a long pause that H. 3d
answered, 'I don't have Judge Krink anymore. He's got table
manners.' "

I suppose a great many people reading the warm little piece
at their breakfast tables had a warm little laugh over its skillful
wistfulness, and in subsequent years I have laughed at it myself. I would like to get together with the judge someday and
forgive him for letting me down, and if I can find Fourace Hill
where I told Heywood he lived, we will get together and throw
butter pats and rolls at each other and dare anyone to try and
stop us.

Anyway, the judge went off into the shadows and I went on
into the dining room and the other places where freedom so
tiresomely reigned.

I hadn't long assumed my new duties when I discovered that
there was truth, not useful truth but truth, in Wilde's line
about the rudeness of gentlemen.

At some gathering or other an unfortunately arch guest
seeking something to say to the solemn kid wandering through
the crowd hailed me with "And whose little boy are you?" I
got a good deal of this kind of thing along with the crushers
like "Are you going to follow in your daddy's footsteps?" and
perhaps this was the second or third time that day that someone had poked me with a conversational stick. Whatever the
cause, I looked up coldly and answered, "You know goddamn
well whose little boy I am."

You'd think this would be followed by shocked silence and
a thunderous order of banishment to my room—not a bit of it.
The remark was laughed at, applauded, repeated, and eventually, slightly softened as to wording, appeared, I believe more
than once, in the *Reader's Digest,* although what wholesome
moral the *Digest* was pointing out I don't know.

Back upstairs I puzzled about this odd aspect of adult life
and I'm afraid that for a couple of weeks I played "The Man

Who Came to Dinner" in search of additional approval. Somewhere in that stretch I am reported to have said that the cure for some ailment of Heywood's was to "Hit him over the head with a cocktail shaker," but the rest of these flights are buried with a lot of early missteps that rise to my mind only in those half-awake hours when time and sense are suspended and what used to be called goblins give you a hard time.

• •

Heywood had a hard time with rudeness. Terrible in his turret of typewriter keys, he smiled charmingly even at people who had roused his deepest anger. I remember how proud he was at having managed to refuse a handshake to Congressman Martin Dies after a session in which he had yielded nothing to the Dies Committee on Un-American Activities in Washington.

"There he was with a big smile and a hand out," reported Heywood, "saying, 'Well Mr. Broun, we certainly had a lively session.' I walked right by without saying anything," this comment in the proud tone of one who expects a commendation rather than the more natural damper from me of "What else could you do?"

Once when he and Westbrook Pegler were locked in struggle across the columns of the *World-Telegram,* Peg had let some personal nastiness wriggle through his column so that I felt justified in cutting him in the corridor of a train bound for Saratoga. Later that night when Heywood was exceptionally late in returning to our hotel room, he replied to my "Where have you been?" with "I was out drinking with Peg."

The snubbing of Gene Tunney, that odd reversion to the club-man character of Heywood Cox Broun, is almost the only occasion of that kind I can remember and was even stranger because Heywood liked Tunney and spent a good deal of time with him talking about sports, which remained a considerable preoccupation of Heywood's long after he quit covering them. One of the things his soberer radical friends deplored was Heywood's well-publicized interest in horse racing. His love of the track had nothing to do with that destructive side of his nature that made him for much of his life a compulsive and not very successful gambler. There was a psychiatric theory that he expressed at the poker table a suppressed sadism, although the fact that he lost more often than he won suggests that the sadism was also repressed by a lot of four-card flushes and unfilled inside straights. I knew him to blast money away on tables he knew to be rigged, and I remember an occasion at a nightclub in New Jersey where the proprietor, hearing that a famous newspaperman was taking a beating at one of his crap tables, walked up and suggested that he throw the dice for the club's distinguished guest. After a remarkably few rolls he said significantly, "You're about even now, aren't you, Mr. Broun?" This elicited no gratitude and the famous, foolish journalist told his wondering son that he was very upset about having to leave when the action was just beginning.

It's true that a good run of cards got us into the house on Eighty-fifth Street, but it was, I've been told, a bad run at cards that got us out of it and on our way, with drays and barrels, to apartments where no helpful Cousin Helens were there to sweep away the excelsior.

Where a Heywood anxious to show his toughness would solemnly push large stakes out on the green felt at a table-stakes game, his racetrack bets rarely exceeded five dollars, and he was not above splitting a two-dollar ticket on some remote possibility described in the handicapper's rundown as "Better off in barn."

He liked to have four or five horses in each race so that something was always in contention, and he always bet on gray horses because they were easy to follow. Among his many problems was what I suppose is called "lensophobia," or the fear of having anything from reading glasses to binoculars in front of his eyes. Even an occasionally employed magnifying glass used, when it could be found, for ferreting out phone numbers had to be held at some distance from his face. This was why he preferred writing numbers in the lining of his hat and on the wall from which the phone hung.

That his serious gambling was in fact suppressed sadism, I am inclined to doubt, because of the way it suddenly ended about two years before his death. He announced to me one morning that he was never going to play big-money poker again, and when I asked why, he said, "I lost nine hundred and fifty dollars last night," as if this were some total explanation. I said that he had many worse nights than that and suddenly his face crumpled into a startling misery.

"Yesterday morning I got a check for a thousand dollars from the Book of the Month Club. I hadn't expected it because I'd been paid for the year, but it was a Christmas bonus and a wonderful surprise. I spent all day thinking of enjoyable things to do with it and now it's gone. I don't know, I think if I had lost five hundred or two thousand I would have gone to the next game, but losing almost exactly the amount of the check makes me feel so terrible that I'm going to quit."

And amazingly he did, playing thereafter in quarter-limit games full of those Spit in the Ocean, Baseball, High Low variations that would have caused growls of protest in the old Thanatopsis days of serious nothing-wild-take-that-joker-out-of-the-deck poker.

If there was any sadism in Heywood it was buried too deep to be discovered in the short stretches of analytic therapy that eased but did not eliminate his collection of phobias, but I suspect that he was busy making up for some imagined inner meanness with all those big tips and big smiles. He would give anything for approval except principle or intimacy. He was so charming that few realized the extent of his reserve. It had none of the stiffness we associate with locked-up people. The wall around the inner Heywood was like one of those fuchsia hedges in Southern Ireland. It was so flower-filled, so soft, and so attractive that its impenetrability went unnoticed. His circle was large, but I think the only person he admitted to actual intimacy was Ruth, and in that relationship she was often like a dentist's probe in a hollow tooth, finding and correcting things but causing a good deal of pain.

If Heywood found face-to-face confrontation difficult and took refuge in the typewriter, Ruth, who had difficulty writing, enjoyed nothing so much as a good slanging match.

Support of this theory lies in the putting of Murdock Pemberton in the second house on the Sabine farm. I think Ruth liked to have a male chauvinist nearby. Murdock and his brother Brock, the theatrical producer, thought and talked like the small-town Kansans they had been, but many years in the arts lent a polish to their provincialism so that they expressed their Hiram Hayseed views with the fluency of musical comedy monologists. (An exception was the climax of a long argument between Murdock and Ruth when, challenged to show some proof of male superiority, he urinated over the porch fence and challenged her to do the same. Ruth for once laughed.)

Why Heywood would go to great lengths to avoid an argument while Ruth sought them out with the zeal of a missionary could, by the psychiatrically minded, be paradoxically traced to the same cause, a stern and frightening mother.

Henrietta Brosé Broun with her grande-dame manner seemed a very different sort of person from little Mrs. Annie Riley Hale who fed her fury on rinds, rusks, peelings, and herb tea, while Mrs. Broun nourished her convictions with rum, plum puddings, and acrid cigarettes from Puerto Rico. The two women, of course, hated each other, and as their exceptionally long lives drew on they would comment with pleasure on signs of decline they affected to notice in each other.

"I hope you realize," Mrs. Hale would say to me, "that all that meat" (she would say the word as if she were mentioning something from which maggots would recoil) "is turning your Grandmother Broun into an arthritic cripple."

Later Mrs. Broun would, with a hand admittedly twisted and swollen, be ladling me out some cholesterol-filled mixture and would remark, "If I had to live on the truck your Grandmother Hale eats, I'd rather die."

She had no intention of doing so until many more dishes had passed and she did, in fact, win the mortality game, ninety-four to eighty-five.

Heywood never fought with his mother, although sometimes safely out of earshot he would wish that he had. He recalled over and over, with a persistence that revealed his hurt, the occasion when his mother said approvingly, "Did you see Alexander Woollcott's wonderful line today about the new Barrymore show? He said 'John Barrymore edged through the play like a beautiful paper knife.'"

"Mother," said Heywood (there was no nonsense here about calling her Etta), "I wrote that line."

"Did you, dear?" was the absent reply. "Well, it seemed so witty I guess I just assumed Woollcott had written it."

Heywood then said something overtly good natured that in the best Freudian tradition he never could thereafter remember.

He submitted cheerfully to attacks on his radical views and his deplorable clothes. He never took up the cause of poor Uncle Fritz, although I think he very secretly augmented the old gentleman's meager allowance. His idea of getting back at his mother was a playful column called "My Mother's Bridge Game" in which he wrote, upon noting that several big games of contract bridge had been raided by the police, that she, a winner of innumerable ashtrays, table lamps, and umbrellas at charity drives, might be gathered up in the nets of the law. He finished the piece with the advice "When the police come go quietly. Insist on your one telephone call before they lock you in the cell and don't give your right name, or my record will be used against you."

This last was a reference to his recent arrest in Milwaukee for picketing, an event of which she had remarked that it "served him right and might teach him to go to bed earlier."

In another column he wrote, "When the revolution comes it's going to be a tough problem what to do with her. We will either have to shoot her or make her a commissar. In the meantime we still dine together."

The little apology after the zinger defines all the years in which he tried to please her, and I am awfully sorry that he never knew what she told me so often after his death, that he was always the one she loved best of her three children.

Ruth and her mother dined together not out of choice but because Mrs. Hale did not make any money out of her endless campaigns against vaccination, vivisection, feminism, the economic policies of Theodore Roosevelt—about which she wrote a book—the economic policies of every president thereafter except Calvin Coolidge, and the mingling of the races, or "mongrelism." Neither was there any income from her vigorous campaigns in favor of native American fascism and a diet free of white flour and animal flesh.

Having thus no money, she lived with us a good deal of time. Heywood couldn't stand her and was therefore exceptionally charming to her, winning little moments of occasional approval despite his ridiculous stand on our economic policy.

Ruth fought pitched battles with her all day long. If Ruth got the better of the argument, as on the day when a discussion about "mongrelism" led her to point out that the Hale nose was visible on many faces in the black community, Annie Riley would burst into tears and say that no one loved her.

Ruth would then say, "Oh, for Christ's sake, Mother" (no first names there either), and Annie Riley would go from grief back to rage at the improper and unladylike use of the Savior's name.

Ruth, for all her fanaticism, worried about all her acts and all her relationships. As her brother Richard once said, she was always announcing that there was something she was never going to do, and then doing it. Firmness of speech was her sword against doubt, but since doubt unfairly attacks from all sides, it isn't the best of weapons. Annie Riley, whose doubt quotient lay somewhere between those of Savonarola and Adam Smith, was luckier, but she seems to have shared her luck with only one of her three children, her eldest son Shelton. I don't remember him well, but I knew that he was law clerk to Oliver Wendell Holmes and at an early age on the staff of President Wilson at Versailles. It is one of the wonders of genetic mutation that a person as illogical as Mrs. Annie Riley Hale could produce a person logical enough to satisfy Justice Holmes, but her basic keenness and her basic confidence were her legacy to Shelton. His death, after an unsuccessful operation, inflamed his brother, sister, and mother against the medical profession, and although Ruth was sensible enough to summon competent assistance for my ailments, she tended, except in extreme circumstances, to avoid doctors herself. Heywood's hypochondria, therefore, did not get the sympathetic attention for which he hoped. Ruth told him to forget his ailments, while his mother-in-law would tell him that one of her mixtures of peelings, stems, and chaffs would sweep his troubles away.

Almost as useless as that advice was the recitation, imposed on me by I forget which of them, of the nonsensical verse of Dr. Emil Coue, a Belgian physician, who for a brief stretch of celebrity had a lot of people fighting germs by saying, "Day by day, in every way, I'm getting better and better."

I, under urging, said it a thousand times through coughs,

colds, and fevers. Whether their virulence was abated by an-
tibodies or this dictated optimism, I don't know, but I haven't
recited the line in years.

More suited to my temperament was Frank Adams' varia-
tion, which ran:

> *Every night, when I turn out the light*
> *I say this little verse:*
> *My friends detect in every respect*
> *I am getting worse and worse.*

The assumption of my grown-uppedness, shaky on matters
of bedtime and diet—my meals were constantly augmented
with oils, the fish-liver ones that came in little gold footballs
that on no account should be broken with the teeth, and the
folk medicine ones like olive oil that was poured into me until
I sweated salad dressing—was quite firm in philosophical matters as far as Ruth was concerned, and from age seven or so on
I was either her confidant or her sounding board on a lot of
subjects that are not normally in the preteen interest range. It
was a strange experience and in some ways made me a strange
little boy.

Many years later at a party, Ring Lardner, Jr., speaking re-
trospectively for the community of normal children, told my
wife, "We all hated Woodie. He was eerie, a little kid talking
like some kind of old man." If Lardner found me eerie from a
child's point of view, I wonder what thoughts ran through the
head of B. Charney Vladek, a member of the highest councils
of the Russian Revolution and later a leader of the American
Socialist Party, as he listened to a small boy explaining the
basic principles of socialism. It is the fate of some of us to
remember in blinding and horrifying detail every disgraceful
moment of hours of foolish behavior. The pompous phrases I
used to Vladek stalk through my mind at this moment, and,

though he was extremely kind and patient, I'm sure he wished himself back on some barricade.

Perhaps, however, he viewed me as I have at last come to view myself—with some forgiveness. I did not, after all, send in my own entry to the intellectual track meet that swirled through the world of Ruth Hale and Heywood Broun. They sent a forty-pound competitor out to throw a sixteen-pound shot and not surprisingly, he dropped it.

Sometimes the mixture of child and adult took odd turns indeed, as in the occasions when I played "store" with Frank Adams. F.P.A. had a large and apparently deserved reputation for rudeness, but he was always nice to me. Apparently in playing the game in which the child industriously sells imagined groceries to a grown-up customer, I earned a place in his published diary by setting myself up as a bootlegger and offering him startling bargains in wine and spirits.

I also told the proprietor of the Conning Tower, a man who was receiving in every mail the offered wit of a whole city, jokes that he might care to use. I must say that one of them he reported—the story of a diner's complaint to a waiter that the servitor had his thumb in the soup. The reply "I don't mind. It isn't hot," still seems funny to me.

Once only I had recourse to plagiarism, interrupting a discussion of the troubles of a famous newspaper publisher with the remark that he had been "Hearst by his own petard." This resulted in such a wave of merriment and congratulation that my iron collar of honor grew red hot and I could only cool it by confessing that I had found the line in *Judge* in a piece by S. J. Perelman. Long afterward when we had become friends, Sid Perelman told me that I should have kept my mouth shut, approval being too hard-earned a commodity easily to be surrendered. I doubt if he would have said that if he'd been at the table, however, and I wasn't yet ready for performer's pragmatism.

Set pieces, the sort of thing where the child does a little rehearsed number, are, in their simple and achievable demands, among the joys of childhood. Whether it's "Tell Uncle Ed how the train whistle goes," or at a later age, "Play chopsticks for Uncle Ed," there's no doubt you'll be able to do it and no doubt that Uncle Ed will be extravagant in his approval.

My first set piece was easy enough to do but certainly not the kind of act widely to be found. Shown any photograph of presidential candidate Harding, I would pound on it with my fist and cry "Vote for Debs, Vote for Debs." I don't know whether there was universal approval of my espousal of the cause of the imprisoned Socialist leader, but there was a lot of easy laughter, and it occurs to me now that if more people had taken my advice the world might have become a much better place.

Despite the vigor of my electioneering, Debs got less than a million votes, and I left politics and entered the arts where I, a three-year-old prereader, amazed our guests by picking out, on command, the requested phonograph record from a pile of thirty or forty. Heywood or Ruth would casually ask me for Caruso's "Keep the Home Fires Burning" and after a little shuffling and looking I would produce it even though its red label was identical to those around it. Sometimes the title given would be one I had chosen myself as more appropriate than the one the composer had given. Thus, asked to bring "Go to Bed Tired," I would produce "The Funeral March of a Marionette." By what trick of configuration–recognition I managed this accomplishment I can't now recall, although I still have a shadowy picture of myself going to a stack of records in the corner of the second-floor bedroom—characteristically they seem to have been piled on the floor about fifty feet from the machine —and coming up with "Le Regiment de Sambre et Meuse," a foot-thudding march I can still whistle. The trouble with doing Debs at two and record-picking at three is that it sets a taxing

pace—no more laughs for saying "Looka me faw down," no
more praise for making the right moves in "Pat-a-cake, Pat-a-
cake, Baker's Man. Somewhere up ahead looms the Palace and
there's a lot of polishing and planning to be done on the way.

The person to whom I was so surly about whose little boy
I was may well have caught me just after the failure of some
joke or trick. I don't know whether there have been many small
children who have come down to dinner running over sotto
voce timings of a line, or, it having failed, have wearily gone
back upstairs changing words and rhythms for some later try.

I suppose one reason I was always glad to see Adams—"A
robust child," he called me—was that he could describe a game
in which he was a train passenger and I the conductor, engi-
neer, waiter, and porter as "such a merry game of make-believe
as I had not played in near forty years."

I never met the children he subsequently had, but I hope he
did as well for them as he did for me.

I soon graduated from selecting other people's songs to per-
forming my own and by the age of nine had a very pretty
repertory of boy soprano numbers ranging from "Rolling
Down to Rio" to a Gregorian chant about the birth of Jesus that
I sang in Oxford Latin.

It is probably too late, or perhaps too unimportant, to bring
psychiatric probing to bear on the question of where the relentless showing off began. Was it the perfectionist parents,
endlessly shaping a Renaissance child? Was it the puny, sharp-
faced little boy hungry for attention and fighting for it? The
sharp-faced little boy thought it was terrible that he should
sing at a party where Paul Robeson, Ed MacNamara, or Richard Hale had headed the bill. He also thought it was terrible
when, after he had grown a little bigger, his voice broke after
he had just learned from his uncle a number called "Our Cook
He Is a Very Dirty Man," a number with which he had scored
heavily no matter who was heading the bill.

As the characters in the popular fiction of that time escaped the pressures of their world by Rolls-Roycing down to the Riviera, so I escaped the pressures of the first and second floors by clopclopping down the stairs to the kitchen where Mattie, to my pleasure, treated me as a very ordinary child whose principal interests were likely to be food and the funnies in the *Daily News,* both of which she always had ready for consumption.

She was brisk with me, and when I burst into tears at some check to my wishes she would remark mildly, "Well, the more you do of that, the less you'll do of something else." This comparison of my towering grief to urination would make me so angry, that like Annie Riley in the face of Ruth's profanity, I would forget to cry. The difference was that no unexhausted clouds of emotion hung over the subsequent scene. Mattie accepted all of my erratic behavior without surprise. I was, after all, at a stage of development somewhere between the brighter pigs and the slower chimps and she found nothing out of the ordinary in my messy consumption of lunch with a mixture of forks and fingers while I tried to read Harold Teen through the blobs of food I had dropped on the newspaper. There were, of course, some basic rules. What I spilled on the table she would clean up, but if I spilled on the floor—highchair behavior, in other words—I had to get a rag and wipe it up myself.

Earl, whose views were somewhat more hierarchical than Mattie's, used sometimes to protest that mopping up wasn't a proper pastime for a crown prince. I used to think then, and still do, that Earl's concern for princes arose from the fact that he was so kingly himself. A tall man of elegant bearing, he spoke standard-stage English in a perfectly produced baritone voice—he was the only person in the house who met Ruth's standards of speech—and he frequently left us for professional engagements that used more of his talents than we could.

At one stretch he was a high priest in an African musical drama by Otto Harbach called *Golden Dawn* which, had it succeeded, might have launched a successful theatrical career. Much later he left us to accompany Jascha Heifetz on a world tour as valet and factotum. He might have kept this job longer if people were not always mistaking Heifetz for Earl's valet and factotum. The master-and-man relationship never really recovered from an occasion when, shortly after a stop in London had afforded Earl a chance to get some Saville Row suits, an Austrian dining-car steward asked Heifetz when his Highness the Rajah would care for his luncheon and was Heifetz going to be privileged to share it with him.

He came back to us in time to teach me to drive a huge old Lincoln roadster that he and I jointly owned and that required twelve precisely timed steps in order to change gears.

In the early years when he had first married Mattie and come to stay with us, he seemed to feel, or pretended through kindness to feel, that I was the most remarkable person he knew, and although I knew he was wrong, I never disabused him.

If he had behaved that way to Heifetz, he might have become an impresario instead of suddenly and finally leaving all of us because of the grotesque and mistaken belief that the faithful Mattie was unfaithful to him.

The only demand that Mattie made of me was that I stay out of her way while she was doing complicated things in a kitchen full of primitive gear that made the boiling of an egg dependent on building a fire in a cast-iron stove. I spent hours sitting in this warm room chattering the kind of twaddle that the child psychologist Jean Piaget once so tellingly described as "The Group Monologue," the conversation that requires an apparent listener but not necessarily a rational response. Mattie pretended to listen, gave me the short answers that her occupation with a lot of work dictated, and blessedly made me forget that I had any obligation to be interesting.

Her basement realm was to me a kind of Switzerland compared to the chaotic kingdoms of the first and second floors where Ruth and Heywood went through emotional swings concerning problems I didn't know existed, and from time to time, because of these swings, sent me suddenly off to the MacKnights after assuring me unconvincingly that I wasn't being banished because of anything incorrect in my conduct.

I asked Mattie whether she knew why I was going, but she would always say diplomatically that it was so I would have a good time, and when I said I knew I wasn't going to have a good time, she would tell me to wait and see.

It was at the MacKnights that I was fitted out with a little riding suit that I hated and, looking in my red-topped boots like a stuffed olive on a leather-topped table, was perched on a horse as sluggish as he was large, and given my first equitation lessons. I don't remember enjoying the lessons, but I have spent a good deal of my life since then on and around horses and I suppose I should send some grudging gratitude back over the years, although I haven't forgiven the suit.

Maybe it was after one of those unwanted trips to the MacKnights, or maybe it was just because I was sent too early to bed, or for some other now forgotten grievance that I forgot my taboo against anger and got mad enough at Ruth to announce, as children frequently do, that I wished for her death.

I am told that in large families where these wishes are constantly shouted it occurs to people after a while that since nothing much happens as a result of the shouting, such terrifying talk is an acceptable form of steam release.

My anger seems mostly to have occurred when I was at the MacKnights, and I can literally recall only two occasions when Ruth and Heywood, once each, lost their tempers with me. Both were times when I wouldn't go to bed. In Heywood's case this resulted in a shoveling wallop that sent me halfway toward the stairs, in Ruth's an actual multiblow spanking for which, confusedly, she apologized the next day.

"If I can't control a five-year-old without beating him, I'm doing something wrong," she told me, and the fact that I remember both times so vividly shows how subterranean and civilized was anger at our house most of the time.

When I burst out at Ruth, therefore, I was invoking magic, and terrifyingly it seemed to be working, as she was struck down by a serious case of diphtheria. Because of the antivaccination zeal she shared with her mother, she had never been inoculated against it and, of course, neither had I, so that I was not allowed in her room. I suppose the fact that this was a children's disease reinforced my guilt about what I supposed I had done, and I hung about her door in dumb misery. Why had I not gotten it instead so I could pay for my badness by dying?

As she began to get better I was relieved of fear, but filled with caution. I must control my powers, and talking to her from the other side of the door during her convalescence I was as full of good intentions as a seminarian—and as incapable of carrying them out as all seminarians save those who become saints.

Of course, I got angry again, and of course the single incident didn't change my whole nature, but I did find that increasingly I used as my weapons not the cannon of honest rage but the pin pricks of sarcasm and the sandbag of sullen withdrawal. At about twenty-six, also a peak age for prizefighters, I developed what I called "good-natured raillery" into an acid-throwing that has created lifetime enemies and brought even understanding friends to tears.

My most common piece of psychological alchemy, however, was my transmutation of hot rage into cold politeness. Aping the courtly cutting edge that Ruth employed at "A-gentlemen-is-never-unintentionally-rude" moments, I got very good at closing doors on efforts to reach me.

Almost half a century after I had wished Ruth dead and had watched my magic almost work, a psychiatrist said to me, "Mr. Broun, do you know how often you use the image of the door? The other side of the door, behind the door, closing the door, I closed the door, they closed the door, and so on?"

Well, yes, I did, and I do, and as I count them, the number of doors real and metaphorical available to Ruth, Heywood, and me, is an infinite stretch like the vision in a pair of facing mirrors.

•   •

A whole new bunch of doors became available when Heywood, for reasons never stated, bought the place down the road from Ruth's and Murdock's houses.

When the first son of the founder, Mr. Holly, was old enough to start a family, Murdock's house was built for him, and the next generation built the place that Heywood so pointlessly acquired. I suppose he hadn't liked all the nose-rubbing of Ruth's highly developed property sense—all that Sabine Farm, Hale Lake, *my place* business—but buying still another house was hardly the most sensible answer, particularly because the first place, after its preliminary fix-up, was still in need of a great deal of expensive work to make it more than a bivouac area. The kitchen was still a shed loosely adhering to the back wall of the house from which only Mattie's magic was able to produce acceptable meals, and the wasp-infected toilet was so far from the main building that the wasps seldom managed the journey. The little building was known as the "Ben Greet," a name I incuriously accepted, only discovering by chance many years later that Greet was a famous English producer of outdoor theater. We were sophisticated enough not to call it the "Chic Sale" after the author of a highly successful book of privy jokes, but not sophisticated enough to eschew our own privy joke.

In the first years of the Sabine Farm the spartan arrangements didn't keep the guests from swarming out from the city.
Every weekend the six little bedrooms were full.

We were still using a bucket on a chain as a water supply,
but when several city guests, mistaking the well for some kind
of garbage chute, dropped the fatty ends of Mac's steaks in it,
some of our remaining rats made the mistake of going after
them.

The appearance in the bucket of a couple of rodent corpses
led to the hasty installation of a more modern water system,
although the "Ben Greet" was not replaced for a couple of
years.

Until I got a horse with its attendant flies even the barn was
used as a sort of dormitory and was occupied all of one summer
by Mildred Gilman and husband and a bachelor friend, Harry
Hatcher, who had a turn for carpentry and made the old place,
if not livable in any modern sense, at least water-resistant.

It seems odd now that so many elegant people were prepared
to rough it in a farmhouse (Frank Case of the Algonquin complained to his daughter Margaret that there seemed to be only
one towel, hanging from a nail and appearing to have been left
by the previous owners) but they came, if not for solace in their
troubles, for the company, the extension of Marc Connelly's
"We-all-loved-each-other" gregariousness to a rural setting.

One of the great pastimes of this group was displaying freedom from convention and in aid of this there was a new convention, compulsory nude bathing in the leaf-mold-clouded
waters of Hale Lake.

Actor Roland Young, one of the more reluctant strippers,
was shocked by lightning during a swim and wondered later
whether it would have happened had he been wearing a bathing suit.

Still as the group grew older, more prosperous, and therefore
more interested in the things that prosperity buys, what a

country house like ours needed was a step up in amenities and what we got instead was another house in only slightly better shape than the first two.

We were now a family of three that owned four houses and lived in three of them. What a lot of doors that was to open and close! What hurtful decisions had to be made about who was staying where, and were those not there left behind or being independent in their choice. This, of course, didn't apply to me since I went where I was sent and managed to feel left behind, outside the door, almost all of the time.

What did they think? What did they say to each other? I never heard anything but the surface stuff about the bargain the new house had been, and how we'd really all be together anyway, and wasn't it really going to be sort of cozy, and all the things that splintered against the reality of separate houses.

Of course, Heywood had outdone his father who had never owned two houses at one time—although weirdly like his father he was soon to have the financial reverses that would make the sale of the town house essential.

There was a good deal of confused moving back and forth between the two country houses because the presence of carpenters and plumbers in one or the other dictated the moves; and the piecemeal episodic nature of the work, dictated by limited resources, made the schedule of moving hard to predict. Another factor was that neither house could function at all without the presence of Mattie and Earl, so where they were was where we had to be.

The big outdoor project was the dredging of the swamp behind Heywood's house so he could have a lake too. It was completed but never given a name and for some reason never swum in.

It was picturesque as viewed from the house and eventually was lined with golf balls that Heywood had failed to drive across it to the little hill that separated his lake from Ruth's.

So the coming together and the flying apart continued, and it wasn't so long after Heywood's purchase of the country house that the house on Eighty-fifth Street was sold, and the uneasy balance of separate existence under the same roof, that strange, unnatural, substantially successful compromise, came to an end.

I cannot now remember where I was when that end came. Perhaps I was away at school or perhaps I have taken refuge in a kind of amnesia. Maybe it was during one of my two summers at Camp Bob White in Massachusetts. Those summers were so successful that they blot out everything else in my memory of the times. They were a pair of two-month stretches in which I felt unrelievedly and gloriously successful. So outstanding a camper was I that, after a summer in the cabin of the Quails, I skipped the Squirrels and became a Silver Fox. If I had been allowed to go back I would have risen to the level of the Bears, and perhaps it was the shortage of funds betokened by the sale of the house that kept me from that ambition.

It was on my return from that second summer that I found Heywood, whether in the house or out of it, in poor shape after a fist fight with his old friend Joe Brooks.

Brooks was as big a man as Heywood and, owing to a devotion to racquet games, in much better shape. As Heywood told it, Brooks had been teasing songwriter Howard Dietz at a party, and seeing Dietz' discomfort, Heywood told Brooks to cut it out. Brooks laughed and Heywood then demanded the fight. Both men took off their dinner jackets and one punch finished the fight, a straight right that broke Heywood's nose and blackened his eye. The protagonists put their coats back on and Brooks left. Heywood then discovered that he had on his conqueror's coat and that it contained a well-filled and precious address book.

Heywood's long-range revenge lay in tearing up the book and throwing it out the window, first passing the torn pages to Dorothy Parker who read the more indiscreet addresses aloud.

It is a tribute to Heywood's charm that Ruth and I forgave him for selling the house and that later Brooks forgave him for the loss of his social life by lending him a lot of money.

Certainly the sale of the house was a sudden decision. Mac-Namara, as was so often the case, was living with us at the time and went off to work in a movie being shot uptown with no notion that a hot dinner and a cold drink would not be waiting on his return.

What he found was a dark house with his trunk at the foot of the stairs and a note on top of it giving a phone number to call. He called it and got Heywood who announced, "I forgot to tell you—I sold the house." Thus was Mac saved from the fate of old Firs in *The Cherry Orchard.*

I suppose one of the reasons I became, in later years, a relentless accumulator of books, pictures, bric-a-brac, and broken bits of this and that to which some memory is attached is that I am probably trying to reestablish the happy clutter of my lost nest.

Looking up at this moment I see six volumes of a high-toned English series of children's books. They are in battered condition and I am not so besotted with nostalgia as actually to read them, but once, in the bookshelf Ruth painted for me, there was *Joy Street,* volumes I through VI, and there are no negative markings in this bunch to prove that they belonged to someone else, although somone else has removed a number of pictures.

If anyone has my copy of *Treasure Island,* the one the Mac-Knights' dog chewed up so badly, I'd like to have that back too, along with the big, broken-skulled doll that received through the hole in its head so many of my youthful confidences.

Sometimes I walk past the house in Eighty-fifth Street—the block is little changed—and wonder why the front steps were removed and what it's like inside. It is a house of small flats now and once in the days when landlords still solicited trade, one of them was advertised for rent, and I thought of taking a look just as a means of getting inside.

I think I was wise not to try, since the sense of loss, dim now but still occasionally popping up in dreams, would just be refreshed and not to any particular purpose.

The two-house system set up in Stamford was copied on a smaller scale in New York, and such stuff as was salvaged from Eighty-fifth Street was divided between two apartments in the same neighborhood. They had to be close together so Mattie could get easily from one household to the other, and the prickly question of where I was to live was put aside for a time by sending me to boarding school in Arizona.

•　　•

The three years I spent at the Arizona Desert School for Boys in Tucson bulked very large in my cosmic self-pity number. "Talk about busing!" began one of the better bits. "It took three days on the train to get to school, and there was no nonsense about coming home for Christmas." It was, in this interpretation, another in my series of long-distance rejections, a trip like that those other trains used to take across the heavens in the *Book of Knowledge.*

When at last I was recounting my go-away grievances to a psychiatrist, he spoiled things (as they so often do) by remarking, "You do a good deal of complaining about the school in Arizona, but you seem to have had a very good time there."

And, of course, I did. There was a pretty terrible first morning when I woke up not in a cozy Pullman berth but in a little white unidentifiable cell, but Miss Thomas, the school nurse, was cruising the corridors listening for new-boy sniffles and soon had soothed away my sobs. By afternoon I was running up and down the aisles of N. Porter's Saddlery, picking out spurs, silk neckerchiefs, and all the things that would make me

one with Hoot Gibson, Tom Mix, Jack Hoxie, and Ken Maynard, the men who galloped so satisfyingly across the screen
at Bim's Eighty-second Street Theater, their horses pacing in
time to bass piano chords. Soon in glorious reality I would sort
of be one of them.

While I was sorting over Porter's dream stuff another blow
was struck at my theory of the "little boy nobody cared for,"
because the store manager came up to announce that there was
a New York phone call for a Woodie Broun. Ruth and Heywood, who couldn't get together on one house, had gotten to
one telephone and gone through all the difficulties of a cross-
country call in the "I-can't-hear-you-operator" thirties to find
out how I was bearing up. As far as I can remember none of
the other boys were so honored, but I, of course, was unap-
preciative because I was in the middle of some big decision
about spur rowels and was inattentive and hurried.

Tucson was a town of 24,000 and the whole state, with a
population of less than 100,000, was an unpaved and beautiful
wilderness still clinging to its identity as the Wild West and
with no knowledge that it was doomed to disappear under the
driveways of millions of middle-management retirees and the
malls that would serve the shopping needs of those millions.

Almost all the students at ADS were in some way sickly,
mostly with what have since been diagnosed as possibly psy-
chosomatic illnesses like asthma. The halls of the school were
often filled with the acrid smoke of burning cowheels, or what
smelled like burning cowheels, which the afflicted used to fire
up in saucers when the ailment was on them.

I was no more than generally unpromising in health matters
but managed in the hot, dry desert air a three-year series of
head colds that puzzled everyone. The psychiatrist was non-
committal (as they so often are) on my theory that I generated
these colds to prove that I needed the chill, wet climate of New
York City.

The school felt that a sound mind in a sound body would be achieved by outdoor classes in the morning and what the Victorians used to call horse exercise in the afternoon, a phrase that leaves it a little vague as to who is getting the exercise and who benefiting from it.

Our outdoor classes (sunshine was still considered an unmixed blessing) were interrupted from time to time when rattlesnakes glided out of the ventilators in the building walls in search of the same warming rays that were presumably doing wonders for us. These excursions did nothing for their health because we were allowed to down books and kill them. These bouts of savagery shot a lot of holes in my grasp of geography, a class that occurred just about at serpentine emergency time, and my knowledge of principal exports is buried under confused pictures of shouting boys and doomed, buzzing snakes.

Continuing the pattern of retreat and advance, like dancers in an old-time reel, Ruth and Heywood, having at great expense sent me to a faraway place, went to great expense to come out and spend the ten-day spring vacation with me. While other boys went on camping trips with the teachers or visited relatives in California, I went to Agua Caliente with my parents and in the great days of that Mexican racetrack discovered the joys of the turf. I collected my winnings in silver dollars and stuffed them in a cloth bag that our luxury hotel had designed for the shining of shoes. When my winners shot under the wire I pounded the bag triumphantly on the handsome table from which we ate our luxurious lunch during the races.

I ended the vacation a hundred dollars to the good and finding that much silver a little awkward to carry, traded my shoebag for a single bill from which smiled the face of Benjamin Franklin, patron saint of thrift.

Shown to school cronies, the magic C-note added vastly to my standing and though I have lost that sum many times in the

less magic years since then, I wouldn't trade all the losses for
the joys, however temporary, of that time in which I thought
I had the world on a string.

•   •

When my school years ended I usually returned to Stamford
rather than to whatever pair of apartments from which Ruth
and Heywood were visiting each other.

Which house in Stamford was another matter, although
after Heywood added a big stone room to his house, a room
so large that the original structure looked like a shed for the
storing of the stone room's firewood, we tended more and more
to stay in his house.

The changes of house may have caused interesting neurotic
patterns in me, and were certainly indicative of interesting
neurotic patterns in Ruth and Heywood, but to the dogs it was
just a case of simple confusion. They were always going up or
down the road to check on the empty place to see if there was
any possibility of a second feeding.

The leader of our pack of two was Captain Flagg, named for
the character in Laurence Stallings' play *What Price Glory?* Ruth
had acquired him in a manner that only she could have thought
up. She had gone to the Speyer Animal Hospital in New York
and asked which was the most miserable and alienated animal
in the group they had available for adoption. She was shown
a big Airedaley-looking creature with a smooth fox hound
head who had been running in circles and whining and starv-
ing himself for several days since he had been brought in off
the street, obviously suddenly separated from a beloved master
or mistress. Ruth and the distressed dog were taken to a waiting room where she sat and he continued his running and
whining. What they both thought about for the next several
hours is not clear, but she was patient until suddenly in the
middle of a running circle the dog stopped in front of her and

put his head in her lap as a signal of a change of fealty.

She took him home to the Eighty-fifth Street house where he signalled his fealty by pinning Heywood to a bed and growling in a menacing manner as an indication that no one was to touch his new friend.

Heywood, who was afraid of elevators, rooms too small and rooms too big, crowds, and cars was surprisingly quite cool and brave in this dilemma. He lay calm and still while Flagg debated tearing out his throat, and when Ruth got the dog off him, said nothing about getting rid of him.

Flagg eventually provided him with a large number of columns and they became friends in a limited way, as Flagg and I did. Mattie and Earl, purveyors of food, stood a little higher than Heywood and I, but the deal he made with Ruth in the Speyer waiting room was the only one he cared about in the twelve years he lived with us.

If Ruth's way of acquiring a pet was the vulnerable looking for the vulnerable, Heywood's was the casual system of feeding strays and then, mildly surprised that they didn't depart, accepting their presence until someone more practical than himself took them away.

The dog Pacifist who preceded Flagg arrived in some haphazard manner and got his name because he was so gentle and sweet. With his little-friend-of-St.-Francis nature, however, went a passivity that made it difficult for him to get up and go outside when hygiene dictated that he should. I think it was Mattie who eventually led him away to the Humane Society over Heywood's half-hearted protests.

Later when he had a penthouse apartment on West Fifty-eighth Street, he acquired a cat named Marian that came over the wall from another building.

"One saucer of milk and on your way," said Heywood. A litter of kittens later, the place was hard to stay in on a hot day, and I often think Ruth and Heywood moved to two apartments on West Sixty-seventh Street to get away from Marian.

All this while, with her usual witless patience, the dog Pandora, Flagg's only other real friend, has been waiting for me to say something about her.

She was a racing greyhound, retired for what reason I don't know and given to me by some sporting friend of Heywood's on the grounds that a boy needs a dog the same way he needs a fishin' pole and a bike, both of which I already had.

Pandora's only ingenuity was in the opening of garbage cans, whence her name, and she was otherwise as dull as she was beautiful. She and Flagg, however, loved each other with a passionate unconsummated love and when, twice a year, she went to the vet during her periods of heat so that he should not sunder her narrow loins with big-headed puppies, he was almost as forlorn as he had been at Speyer Hospital, although he didn't go so far as to starve himself.

If you saw me in those far-off days with my dog, my bike, and my rod, you could well have put me down as a real Norman Rockwell cover boy, a barefoot youth on his way to the crick with no more cares than the problem of where to find night crawlers for bait.

If you had asked me at the time what I resembled, you would have gotten a picture of something half out of J. S. Le Fanu, the Gothic master, and half out of Krafft-Ebing. The list of my sins seemed to grow every day and I forgot none of them, however trivial.

If you had asked Ruth and Heywood where I stood on the scale between the Rockwell boy and the feeble master of my imaginings, I haven't really any idea. Or rather, there is a single idea. I knew from what they gave me to read and from the way we talked among ourselves about a variety of things that they thought I was smart. Were you to ask the adolescent me whether I had any virtues at all, I would timidly, or very occasionally, arrogantly, offer the large collection of facts that reading and a retentive memory had stuffed into my head.

I imagined myself also to be a reasonably good public performer since they seemed very willing to display me either as
the boy soprano or the midget wit of the dinner table. It may
be that this belief, whether mistaken or no, made it possible
for me to walk, unprepared, into the professional theater at the
age of thirty with a good deal more confidence than anybody
thought I should have.

• •

During all the time I was brooding about what they thought
of me, I naturally gave no thought to what they thought about
themselves. Children are naturally self-centered, only children
are more so, sickly only children are a step further along, and
finally you get to me.

It never, for instance, occurred to me that two complicated
people who were desperately trying to hang on to each other
even as their disparate natures were pulling them apart might
find a small clear-eyed observer a distraction. That they loved
me they proved in every way except those that I was likely to
believe. That my absence was a small weight removed from
their packs of problems came to me too late for me to do
anything grown-up or generous about it.

It was Heywood who introduced me to the work of P. G.
Wodehouse, a splendid change from his usually inexplicable
favorites and, ungratefully, I found my role model in Jeeves.
I did not pretend to the great man's omniscience and unfailing
ability to solve the most complex of problems, but the manner,
the cool remoteness, seemed just what I had been looking for.
I practiced shimmering in and out of rooms. Always polite, I
tried to give the impression that I knew a great deal more than
I was saying, and I worked on a smile that was superior without being presumptuous.

A child psychologist probably would have said, "The boy is

in danger of withdrawing into a world of very limited emotion." I preferred to think that I was on the top floor of my castle with the drawbridges up and that if the whole of Quentin Durward's Scottish Archer Guard and all the servants of Dr. Fu Manchu asked if they could come upstairs and have a talk about my recent misdeeds, I could give them the horselaugh, or like Lon Chaney in *The Hunchback of Notre Dame* (a character with whom I felt a close kinship) I could pour disagreeable things like hot lead on any who did not get my message and move off.

Heywood in particular took my Jeeves act very hard. Himself a master of remoteness, he liked to do the withdrawing, and would get visibly nervous when I went into my shimmer and my smile. I don't know how many hundreds of people have said to me over the years that from reading his column they felt they knew him well, and there is no doubt that he could, from his typewriter, radiate intimacy like a fifty-thousand-watt transmitter.

When it came to father and son talks his wattage was neutralized by the simple fact that he was going from monologue to dialogue and found it very hard.

I remember many a late night when he would take a deep breath and ask whether anything was bothering me, or how I was getting on at school. I could have replied tartly to the last one that he would know better if he were not always losing my report cards in the mountains of his unanswered correspondence, but as he was genuinely making an effort, I would try to make one too and come to the castle gate with some quickly selected or, if things were relatively okay, quickly made-up problem for us to discuss. Painfully, like two kids at dancing school, we would try to mesh the steps of a good exchange of questions and answers.

Poor Heywood always broke first. Perspiring with embarrassment he would cry, "Are you hungry? Let's make an omelet," and rush off to the kitchen to mix anything short of poison with a bowlful of eggs. I'm not even sure about the poison. Once he made us an anchovy-marmalade omelet that, if not lethal, proved disturbing well into the next day.

On another occasion, observing a melancholy that shone through my normal impassivity, he took me out to lunch and invited me to open my heart. Touched that he had noticed, I produced a photograph of myself and the girl whose absence was graying my world.

Admittedly the snapshot was somewhat overexposed, but it seemed clear to me that it was a picture of a rather ordinary-looking college freshman with his arm around the most beautiful girl in the sophomore class. She having transferred to another college, it seemed to me that my life had early reached its high point and now stretched before me as a downhill run to the grave.

Heywood's question, "What are you doing in drag?" struck me like an obscenity shouted in the middle of a hymn. I was too stunned to be immediately angry, although in later months I seethed over this insensitivity as a kind of counter-irritant to my heartbreak. After I had explained the true nature of the picture we might still have had a satisfying talk about the rise and fall of my hopes of happiness if he, Heywood, had not compounded the injustice by asking, "Isn't this the same girl whose picture you showed me last year?" There was a pause as some part of the luncheon arrived and we finished the meal on the safe ground of a discussion of the prospects of various candidates for the Belmont Stakes, horse racing being the subject with which we filled many awkward stretches.

Saddest of all our father and son talks began with an invitation to the races.

"How would you like a trip to the track?" he said one bright Stamford morning. His voice was so full of artificial bonhomie that, had I been younger, I might have thought it was a ruse to get me into the car for a trip to the railroad station for still another send-away, but this seemed an unlikely ruse to practice on an eighteen-year-old so I accepted. Heywood's nervousness lasted through the whole race card, a subsequent dinner at "21," an evening at *Earl Carrol's Vanities,* and a trip to a now forgotten nightclub where he started several times with the kind of throat clearing that foretells a major message, only to end by asking the waiter for another drink.

At five o'clock in the morning, nineteen hours after we had started on this round of fun, he put his chopsticks on the table of an all-night Chinese restaurant and husked out a rather cloudy statement with an interrogatory rise at its end.

"I don't know if you've had anything to do with girls," he said, and after a moment or two of debating whether he meant dancing, kissing, or vowing eternal love—all of which I had done—I correctly decided that this was a query about my virginity.

In an indignant tone that hid my disappointment I admitted my inexperience and Heywood, looking down into his plate, said that he imagined that I was worried about my performance as a lover and that he wanted to tell me that not everybody was good all the time—that when you were with someone you loved and who loved you it would somehow be all right no matter what.

Left out of this account are a lot of pauses, meaningless murmurs from me, and a good deal of euphemism and evasion. Still the message had been given and, for a shy person who cherished a reputation as a lady's man, at grindingly painful cost.

In subsequent years I have sometimes had occasion to doubt whether what he told me was true, but the wisdom of the advice isn't the point. And that awful long day when he had to pick horses, pick dinner dishes, and sit through the colorful inanities of theater and cabaret, while endlessly rewording his message and wondering whether it would do more for me than refresh the contempt he was sure I felt for him, must have seemed to him not like nineteen hours but nineteen days while a jury debated his case.

In practical matters Heywood was as fluent as Lord Chesterfield and a good deal less pompous. When I was fourteen he began my financial education. While Ruth, who had announced that "A Gentleman must know how to dance, drive, and play bridge if he is not to be a dead weight at a weekend party," was taking care of the bridge, and Earl was teaching me to drive (nobody ever taught me to dance, as a number of partners were later to discover), Heywood told me that men who embezzled company funds or took the childrens' education money to back sure things at the track or in the market were simply people who had not had the responsibility of handling money in their early years and had never learned that there were no sure things.

He therefore opened for me a bookmaker's account with one of the telephone men in the Frank Erickson gambling empire and gave me a small capital with which I was to trade in ten-share lots in the stock market. I was to pay my losses out of my allowance and whether I succeeded or failed was to remember that money had only one purpose. It was to spend. Too many people took pleasure in piling it up for the simple pleasure of counting it. "Try to be rid of it by the end of the week when your employer will give you a fresh supply," he said, "and when you are old enough to have a checking account, don't bother with filling out all those little stubs. The bank is very good at letting you know when you are out of money."

Various sure things failed at the track at a rate to keep me from going overboard in subsequent years, but the beginning of my Wall Street career, occurring as it did during the historic lows of 1932, was a series of staggering triumphs. Having arrived on the scene at the right moment, I did what lucky people so often do and ascribed my success as an investor to astuteness. The boy who had explained socialism to Charney Vladek was now willing to give the secrets of Wall Street success to anyone who would listen—a group that must have included a number of people who didn't really want to. I was, however, eventually silenced by the bear market of 1936, an event that completed the education Heywood had in mind.

From the beginning, racing made me poorer but happier. The steady drain on my funds was compensated by triumphs of the ego like the day I sent ten football players to the Horace Mann School for Boys senior prom. The players were scholarship athletes from New Jersey high schools and parochial schools and the five-dollar cost of the dance was hopelessly beyond their reach. I suggested that each of them put up a quarter and I would select a 20-1 shot and see if we couldn't bring off a small miracle. When the small miracle came home in front and I distributed five-dollar bills among my happy classmates, a feeling of uncomplicated, unalloyed happiness swept over me that was worth all the weeks in which my available funds went off to the bookmaker's bank account.

It speaks well for this curious educational system that Heywood had devised that I limited myself to what I had. I never borrowed to bet even when I felt that the best bet of the year waited only on my phone call to the Manhattan number that mysteriously was answered from New Jersey.

The man who gambled away his house, son of the man who lost his house in the panic of 1907, had, if nothing else, broken the chain. When Heywood spoke sagely of the men who had no training in youth in the handling of money and were therefore later to be easy marks, he was, of course, speaking of both his father and himself.

Old Mr. Broun, in his constant embellishment of his image as a latter-day George Brummell, ruined himself a couple of

• WHOSE LITTLE BOY ARE YOU? •

times and, as Brummell moved to unfashionable Belgium, so Heywood Cox Broun ended up at an address in Upper Manhattan that he hated to see in his club yearbooks.

Heywood, who bought the house on Eighty-fifth Street out of poker winnings, had to sell it on account of poker losings, the story as it trickled down to me being that a five-thousand-dollar beating in a single night had decided him not to give up poker but to give up the house in order to get a fresh stake.

I suppose what he did with me might be described as the moral equivalent of homeopathic medicine, that system where the patient ingests small amounts of the appropriate infectious material as a guard against the effect of larger amounts.

I was certainly a very active gambler in my high school and college days, betting by telephone on every day when horse-race action was available anywhere in the country and sometimes on a dull Sunday, reaching across the water to wager on the stumbling unpredictable stock that raced at Oriental Park in Havana. Still, in a lifetime of temptation whose figures have been further skewed by inflation, I have never had a day when betting cost me or earned me as much as five hundred dollars. Parental guidance could not hope to achieve any more than that, and I suspect that if Heywood had used the more conventional ploy of a talk about the evils of gaming I might now be throwing my last chip onto some roulette table and waiting for the ivory ball to roll it away.

If I talked to Heywood about money, I talked to Ruth about books and plays and music. When I was in Arizona it was she who sent a monthly half-dozen volumes, chosen with considerable care. Uncompromising in all things, she included no favorites like Tom Swift in the package and I was kept in ignorance as to the progress toward world domination of the villainous Dr. Fu, but then I was probably the only twelve-year-old boy who received Aldous Huxley's *Brave New World* and Homer Smith's *Kamongo,* a dialogue between a priest and a scientist on the nature of the powers that control the natural world. From time to time, to show that she was not a puritan (although, of course, she was) she would include Robert Benchley or Frank Sullivan. On one occasion she sent, for a psychological reason hidden from us all, F. Anstey's *Vice Versa*, a Victorian fantasy about a wretched boarding school boy who avenged himself for his exile by practicing magic on his father in a manner too complicated to be explained here.

Feelings, as psychiatrists never cease telling us, are very different from thoughts, and I always felt that I was less of a disappointment to Ruth than I was to Heywood, despite the fact that it was she who was always correcting my grammar and pronunciation, and whacking me on my narrow shoulders in an effort to get me to stand erect. I thought of complaining that these blows were more trouble than the posture board in Rogersville employed to straighten her up, but remembering how hard it was to win an argument from her, I just stood correctly until I left the room.

I suppose Ruth's constant small criticisms made it at least clear what she wanted of me, and that I could please by throwing back my shoulders, ending sentences with words other than prepositions, and speaking in the manner Hamlet commended to the Players.

To please Heywood, I used to feel I would have to be someone else to start with. Of course, I don't know what he really felt; I only know what I thought he felt, and the constant drumbeat of questions about my height and weight (both unsatisfactory) made it obvious that a larger model would have been much more acceptable.

For the most part I answered these questions in my cool remote manner, giving the desired statistics in a level tone, omitting only the "Would there be anything else, sir?" from my gentleman's-gentleman impersonation. Only once did I break and show natural irritation. I was seventeen and had replied five foot eight and one hundred and twenty pounds to the familiar question that Heywood said with what seemed to me depressing urgency, "Did you ever hear of boys growing much after that age?" "No, I didn't," I cried, dropping my cool like some unwanted overcoat. "This is it. This is what you got. I'm never going to be six-feet tall. I'm never going to be five-feet-nine-inches tall. You'll have to settle for this."

He didn't even look angry and this drove me into a flurry of apology that I didn't really mean and therefore made all the more abject. He never asked about my size again, but then I never got any taller either.

He worried, and told me that he worried, about my shell and admitted that he liked to go to the races with me because it seemed to be the only place where I got excited. I could have told him that in fact I lived in a continual state of excitement, mostly in the form of a series of anxieties, interrupted by complex erotic fantasies involving almost every reasonable-looking girl I saw, by responses to music as if the notes were a scented storm of warm rain, by excitement over ideas old to many but new to me, and by a general feeling that whatever my future, sensational or disgraceful, it would be of interest to millions.

What I actually told him was that I was sorry and that I would try to be more open. I wasn't really sorry because it seemed to me that by keeping my feelings to myself I would be less of a nuisance and demonstrably the independent person they had wanted since they first set me on a telephone book at the dinner table and left me to deal with the witty dinner partners at my left and right.

Many years later a number of people told me that Heywood was fiercely proud of my smallest accomplishments and forced on his friends clippings of my contributions to school magazines and accounts of his own devising of my brilliance in school plays, but since he was as good at withholding his feelings as I was (we dislike in our children those qualities we most dislike in ourselves, said somebody wisely and uselessly), I got no hint of any of this when it would have warmed us both in a festival of giving and receiving.

Nathaniel Benchley, that most civilized of men, who balanced himself with costly aplomb between the fame of his father Robert and that of his son Peter, gently used to take me to task for saying things like those I have just put down.

We used to discuss which was worse, to look like one's father, as he did, or to have the same name, as I did. Neither seemed a good idea, but we came to no firm conclusions nor did I ever find out what he thought about his father. He told stories about Bob but they were admiring set pieces.

Once when my wife suddenly asked Nat at a dinner party what he had thought when he met me, he was caught off guard and said, "I was talking to Heywood, who was instantly making me feel at home, when a sad, alienated-looking boy came into the room and Heywood, his voice suddenly offhand and cold, said, 'You know my son, of course.' " Then he looked stricken at having broken his own rule of civility, but he hadn't broken any rules of reportorial accuracy.

I think Nat was particularly distressed when I said occasional mildly critical things about Heywood because he himself had worked for that odd publication, *The Connecticut Nutmeg*, later, when the other suburban celebrity founders dropped out, to be called *Broun's Nutmeg*, and had found Heywood a paragon of warmth and understanding.

I was twenty at this time and Heywood was making a last effort to mold me to his hopes by employing me on the *Nutmeg*, while bearing up under my constant insistence that such work was irrelevant to my ambition to teach college English.

The Nutmeg was the kind of paper that is dreamed up at a country cocktail party where the fumes of gin mingle with the lilac sweetness coming through the window. This heady blend maddens people into believing that running a small-town weekly is a lot of fun. Possibly it is, but the *Nutmeg,* despite a gardening column and a certain sophisticated rusticity suggestive of jolly times at Balmoral, was a long way from the little papers that thrived on social notes and editorials deploring sanitary conditions at the bus station.

The celebrity proprietors, among them novelists Ursula Parrott and John Erskine, agent Geroge Bye, sports editor Gene Tunney, and foreign correspondent Quentin Reynolds, began dropping off like leaves from a sick gardenia and in no time at all the paper and its deficit belonged wholly to Heywood. The *Nutmeg* found room for some very good pieces by Nat Benchley and for a weekly feature by me that was lavishly and helpfully illustrated by John Groth, but for the most part it was a Heywood Broun festival, some pieces appearing under such pseudonyms as "Blake Hemphill," and more transparently "Howard X. Brown," and a great many under his own name.

Here he reprinted in installments his least successful novel, *The Sun Field,* mysteriously announcing that it was by "Peter Neale," in fact the hero of *The Boy Grew Older.* Here he expressed his opinions without fear of the distorting trims and cuts with which Scripps-Howard was beginning to torment him as a prelude to the termination of his contract a year later. Here he had an uncomplicated good time, alloyed only by the fact that he was beginning to have to borrow money to keep the paper going.

An experienced Stamford newspaperman named Harold Yudain did the makeup and editing, and as the greenhorn of the operation I gave the printers pleasure by unwisely taking in my hand the sticks of hot type they enclosed in galley-paper hammocks and handed to me.

The Nutmeg is as good an illustration as any of a major paradox. On the surface Heywood carefully cultivated an image of slovenly laziness. He pictured himself as a genial sloth raising a hand only to reach for a drink, a late sleeper who breakfasted in bed while reading the funnies, all in all a feeble fribble who had fooled a series of editors into giving him easy jobs.

In fact, of course, he had, however rumpled his clothes and irregular his habits, conducted his column without missing a day, written three novels, produced and acted in a Broadway show, run for Congress on the Socialist ticket, operated a free employment agency—"Give a Job 'Til June"—during the worst of the Depression, helped to found and served as first president of the American Newspaper Guild, and poured thousands of words and dollars into *The Nutmeg*—all this without finding a matching pair of socks, or on some mornings, any socks at all.

Ruth, on the other hand, appeared to be a rocket of energy and had soared successfully through a productive decade. Alert to everything that was happening, precise in speech and thought, she seemed a success machine in excelsis, ready to move into high gear at any moment. No one really knows why the absence of some cog or other kept the machine rumbling in place or limited its successes to the completion of a particularly challenging diagramless crossword or the completion of the clueless blue sky of a giant jigsaw.

It was Ruth who had been the art student and shown promise both as sculptor and painter; it was Heywood who achieved some small fame as an amateur painter. Admittedly he generated some of the small fame himself by announcing his art progress in his column, but he turned out what he always called "Early Brouns" for twenty-five years, and took immense pleasure in doing them.

I sometimes think Ruth gave up art because she suspected a limitation to her talent and couldn't stand to do something that was merely decorative, but Heywood, whose creative ego was invested entirely in his writing, daubed away at his misty landscapes with a simple pleasure in the doing, a Zen archer who had dropped for a time his bow to try a hand at making mud pies.

Early in his career as a painter he gave up brushes because he discovered they were a nuisance to clean, and used pieces of rag to apply his colors, often lying full-length on the grass like some horizontal Monet. Instead of a smock he had a pair of special flannel pants stained as if he had spent a quarter century slapping colors on scenery in a theatrical stock company.

I have a late-period "Early Broun" on my wall that is a head-on view of the skyline of lower New York, and in which, so that the whole foreground will not just be blue-gray water, he has constructed a mysterious bridge. There are no cars on the bridge, which is a good thing because the bridge looks as if the weight of the second car or the first truck would send it crashing into the harbor.

A shrewd and candid judge of painting, the Japanese artist and frame maker Bumpei Usui, shown an anonymous Broun, remarked to me that the man who had done this work was not a painter at all but a poet. Considering that Usui frequently advised his artist clients not to frame their work at all, I felt that Heywood had achieved a tribute he would have appreciated when the picture was allowed to stay in the frame shop.

Arthur Brisbane, columnist and resident intellectual for the Hearst papers, bought one of Heywood's pictures for a hundred dollars, a high-water mark in the Broun market, but this tribute was clouded by the fact that Hearst was trying to interest Heywood in a contract at the time and by the fact that Brisbane never came around to collect the picture.

The critic whose opinion was perhaps the most eagerly sought, Ruth, never, at least in my presence, said a word about any of the canvases, early-early, middle-early, or late-early. Considering that she had views on everything about Heywood from his neckties (or lack of them) to his opinions and the manner in which he expressed them, this may seem strange. Maybe her professional disapproval was too strong to permit expression, maybe she thought he should have one area for what kindergarten teachers call "unstructured play," or maybe she simply did not know what to make of them.

Since Ruth was always the critic, the impatient one, the corrector of grammar and speech, in short the gadfly, you would have supposed when they broke up it would have been Heywood who cried out in protest and demanded surcease and a divorce. In fact, it was Ruth who forced the break.

•   •

They had held together for seventeen years when the break came. Somewhere in the winter of 1933 they began taking hesitant steps toward the dissolution of their marriage, cautious experiments in irreversible freedom. One of the strangest of these was a trial separation in which paradoxically we went on a Caribbean cruise together. Heywood took along, in a decorous separate cabin, his secretary with whom in a conscientiously devil-may-care way he was having an affair; and Ruth, in another separate cabin, adopted the pose that she knew none of us and was a single traveler named Miss Richards.

Meeting by arranged chance on the first night aboard, we had the maitre d' seat us at a table for four. A more ramshackle and self-defeating scheme could hardly be imagined. It paralyzed everyone except me whom it simply frightened. If Ruth wanted to move into a new world, she was sitting at the wrong table; and if she didn't, what was the disguise for? The secretary, a sensible woman whose affair with Heywood I would not have credited had he not insisted on telling me about it, crept around the decks in a state of depressed embarrassment, and I played hundreds of games of shuffleboard.

"Miss Richards," the presumed beneficiary of all this make-believe, was the most wretched of all, a fact I discovered when my casual criticism of her hairstyle sent her to her cabin in tears. I don't think I had ever seen her weep, and horribly aware that once again I had been unintentionally rude, I reported the incident to Heywood and was sent to apologize. The sorries were surprisingly accepted by a strangely soft Ruth who then embraced me with frightening intensity, as if she were the one who was about to be deserted.

Whether out of resentment or carelessness, I shortly blew the cover on the business by saying to a shipboard friend with whom we were having drinks that "my mother" would be joining us shortly. The new friend, a worldly man, remained composed when Ruth showed up, and when I later confessed the gaffe, Ruth was amused. She decided that the man assumed me to be the illegitimate issue of a just-renewed old romance of Heywood's. About the only good anybody got out of that cruise was a barrel of Robbins Island oysters that Heywood received every year from the new friend to whom I had betrayed Ruth's secret.

It seems that the subject of oysters had come up during one of our cocktail-hour meetings and Heywood, for once dropping his pose of gustatory ignoramus, had delivered quite a lecture on the varieties of the species, ending with the flat statement that the king of bivalves was the Robbins Island variety from Maine. The new friend had burst into smiles and applause and revealed that he was a major harvester and shipper of this variety.

It didn't seem to me that Ruth's two weeks of life under the name of the tough old aunt from Culpepper County, Virginia, had made anything all right, but the wheels were already turning and I suppose nothing at that point could have stopped this latest and deepest of their flights from each other. In my constant comings and goings, and as I watched the advances and retreats of their house shiftings, I often equated the three of us with a toy that was popular in those days.

Stapled to a cardboard square were a pair of flat, metal, brightly colored clowns as well as a female bareback rider and horse, a magnet, and a steel sliver. This pin, held at one end by the magnet and attached at the other to the clowns' conical hats or the rider's curls, would permit them to spin precariously at one remove from the mysterious power that joined them.

Simple instructions on the cardboard showed how the power could be reversed to replace or even repel the performers. The only thing it didn't explain was the nature of magnetism, which I still don't understand any more than I do the invisible forces that moved us around. I did not understand it either when Ruth knocked on my door—"May I come in?"—to explain why she was going to get a divorce. The explanation was as quiet and rational and basically terrifying as any of the bad behavior talks of earlier years except this time I didn't have to try to explain anything. It was Ruth's turn. Nothing, I was assured, would change their relationship with me. Nothing really would change in their own relationship. It was just that Ruth, wishing to take up again her journalistic career, felt that this could be better accomplished if she were not operating in the shadow of Heywood Broun. She had thought of doing this much earlier but felt that it would be hurtful to me in the tender years of childhood. Now I was old enough to understand—a curious and meaningless compliment to one who had been treated as old enough for too many things for too long— and she was old enough so that the move had to be made quickly or not at all. It was a wintry sunny day and the apartment, always a draughty place, seemed full of unexpected icy puffs as the steady calm voice kept on with its totally unconvincing claim that the world wouldn't change and that the magnet had not become a lifeless crook of old iron.

I, of course, offered a calm as imperturbable as Ruth's, said that I sympathized with the problem, understood the need for the divorce, and would do whatever I could to ease the transition. I went back to school (I was boarding in Riverdale at Horace Mann), and Ruth went to Mexico for the proceedings. Where Heywood was during this crisis I can't say, but he did the ultimate cool, civilized thing and never discussed it with me at all. I gathered from occasional cracks in his mask that he didn't think much of the idea, and I was never sure that Ruth did.

We were all in the iron grip of freedom, however, and anyone who interfered with freedom was automatically bad. Freedom meant dignity, meant creativity, meant civilization at its highest level. I felt rotten, but I could hardly be against civilization at its highest level, so I worked very hard at convincing myself that the divorce, by freeing Ruth's creative energies, would make her happier and that his would make all who loved her feel better.

Nothing better illustrates the strange nature of this apparent breakup than the story Mattie told me forty years later.

It seems that when Ruth returned from Mexico, Heywood went down to the station to meet her and they returned to go happily and successfully to bed together, something they hadn't done for several years. Mattie said she couldn't make any sense of it, adding with automatic loyalty that she guessed it was just proof again of how special they were, but to me it was further proof of what I had already suspected—despite my moment of despair, the magnet had not lost its push-pull power. This had just been the biggest of the push-pulls and had ended with the little bright figures spinning again at the end of their metal thread.

One change in arrangements shortly after the divorce was that they moved from two apartments seven blocks apart that they had occupied as a married couple to two apartments on

West Sixty-seventh Street that were in the same building.

Here one day we all finally met to talk about the future, specifically in terms of living arrangements. Up to now nothing had ever been regularized and when home from school I had moved among the houses and apartments without much pattern. It hadn't been very satisfactory but it hadn't been traumatic. Now suddenly Ruth and Heywood, dealing uncertainly with their cloudy divorce, had decided to be clear about something—I must decide with which of them I was going to live.

I backed away like a horse faced with a strange stall. Surely, I said—and I was perfectly right—the parents of a sixteen-year-old boy should make this decision and announce it. They were still the authorities.

You might think that by saying authority I had brought something obscene into the discussion. They had taught me better than that, they protested. We were free adults consulting together as we so often had in the past. They were too mature to turn this into a whom-do-you-love-best proceeding and they assumed that I was mature enough to treat this matter as a simple business not of where do I put my heart, but where do I put my clothes and books. This seemed to me to be nonsense, and painful nonsense at that. As it happened, my chair was set between theirs and I could feel an almost palpable pull at my wet, closed fists.

Denying their obvious apprehensions they fell back again into the swamp of reason. We would, after all, be together in the summers on the adjoining Stamford properties and certainly we would continue despite the change in their relationship to celebrate the major holidays at Grandmother Broun's, so what was all this hesitancy about what amounted to picking a hotel room?

Contradicting them firmly just as if I were the equal adult of the family fantasy, I said that I didn't see how a decision favoring one over the other could fail to be hurtful. I didn't want to hurt anybody, I said, and I thought the best solution was the toss of a coin. This was the best idea I ever had and like most really good ideas it was shot down at once. It was frivolous and irresponsible and showed that I didn't really believe what they had said.

With calm detached smiles designed to show that no one much cared what I decided, they pushed me for a decision, and having offered the best solution, I now offered the worst.

Sitting between two people desperately if silently bidding for my fealty, I put my answer on a rational, architectural, nonhuman basis. Since the two apartments were the same except that Heywood's had one small extra bedroom, why did I not opt for that additional cell so that closets would not have to be emptied. In this way, I said, feelings would be spared and we could all live reasonably together.

The smiles didn't waver. No feelings about the choice or the chilly way in which it had been achieved were allowed to surface. Even as the ghostly tugging at my hands slackened, I was congratulated on the intelligence inherent in my choice.

I walked out of the conference with a fool's assurance. I had been Solomon come to judgment, Talleyrand at the Congress of Vienna, a pretty slick article all around. What I had done, of course, was convince them that I didn't care much about either of them, and given Ruth the additional wound of total rejection.

Within a few weeks I heard from Uncle Richard that she had wept inconsolably for days. It seemed that the little boy who had almost killed his mother with magically summoned diphtheria was having another try.

The detached smiles stayed firmly in place, held there by the agonizing nails of self-discipline, so there was no chance for me to change my decision, which might, in any case, simply bring on melancholia in Heywood.

It didn't occur to me that Heywood had been so assiduously

practicing for rejection that he might have been rather relieved to experience the real thing. After all both wife and son had deserted the protagonist of *The Boy Grew Older,* leaving him to rattle the keys of his only real friend, the typewriter. The unmarried hero of his second novel, *The Sun Field,* loses the woman he loves, while Bunny Gandle, in *Gandle Follows His Nose,* chooses always the lonely road that leads not to home but to adventure and possible disaster.

Ruth had divorced him, and there might have been a kind of grim artistic satisfaction in seeing me go out the door after her—except, of course, that none of us going out the door ever let go of the knob on the other side.

I did my short-run best, spending hours down in Ruth's apartment having long, intimate, satisfying talks about everything. We were closer than we had ever been before, but long talks are pale invalid broth compared to the heart's blood that oozes from a primal hurt.

I took refuge, as my guilt grew into a big smothering, wet feather bed, in the idea that they had forced the business on me. I had only done what was asked, and had done so after coming up with a superior chance-governed formula that would have spared everyone's feelings and so forth to no avail. It still came down to the fact that I had not insisted on my right as the child to make them act like parents instead of colleagues. I had gone along with their folly because it was just too hard to deny it without getting down to the roots of all our troubles, a job for which I didn't have the courage.

I should have—I should have—I should have—but I didn't, and when, a year later, Ruth died mysteriously, simply through a gradual weakening and letting go, the should-haves became a heavy weight called "all-my-fault."

Going up and down the elevator between the two apartments I realized very quickly that despite the superficial resemblance, it wasn't like going up and down the stairs at Eighty-fifth Street. There we had had common meeting grounds—the dining room, the kitchen, the pulling together that every family has against alarms and exigencies.

It became rather a relief to go back uptown to school where, a reasonably good student, and a reasonably contented one, I could lose myself in that ancestor of transcendental meditation, the memorization of dates.

In the spring of that year we got out of the two apartments and went to Stamford where everyone lived in Heywood's house, the excuse being that Ruth, needing money, had rented her place as an income-producing proposition.

No one believed that, but it was easier than saying that somehow the new career was not starting and that she seemed not to have the energy to look for ways to start it. The new career, or the resumption of the old career, was not, in fact, ever mentioned again after the divorce, although Ruth kept herself reasonably busy reading and evaluating the Book of the Month Club entries that Heywood would, when properly primed, discuss at the meetings.

Both of them began to drink more, but in a steady quiet way that never led to any staggers, slurred speech, or public embarrassment.

William Bolitho, a writer Heywood much admired, had written that "The shortest road out of Manchester is a bottle of gin." A. E. Housman had put it another way with "Look into the pewter pot and see the world as it is not."

What world Ruth saw when she looked into the amber wineglass of gin and bitters with which she began so many of the last days of her life, I don't know. Certainly it wasn't the new world of which she had talked so much in the days just before the divorce. Maybe it was just the same old world without the unbearable sharpness it had when her critical faculties were working full blast.

Heywood was balancing a fear of death that was constantly

exacerbated by the poking fingers of doctors who all too easily could find and deplore his liver, and the fact that alcohol seemed the prime specific for him for his phobias. He decided fairly early on the bad boy pose that he had used in matters of dress, and was always flourishing his big battered silver flask in places where it was calculated to shock, although when I got him to speak at Swarthmore College's Quaker Meeting House he was sufficiently awed by the good gray atmosphere to fill his water glass with gin in the privacy of the prespeech anteroom.

At Newspaper Guild conventions and on other occasions when long hours of concentration were required, Heywood was always urging his miracle food on his fellow concentrators. This consisted of vanilla ice cream into which canned or fresh blackberries had been puddled with the solvent aid of a glass of gin. The ice cream, according to the dish's inventor, provided sugar for energy; the gin gave steadiness and confidence; and the berries protected the consumer from scurvy.

I don't know how much of this stuff he actually ate but its constant advertisement was a splendid defiance of his heritage of oenological expertise and once again made him a champion. Some of his other occasional mixtures were as odd as the anchovy-marmalade omelet and I should guess, although I never tried them, as unpalatable.

During periods of reform when he was taking long walks in a rubber sweat suit, chopping wood, and making a great parade about limiting himself to fruit juice as part of a drive for fitness, Nat Benchley and I were instructed that when asked to bring him grape juice we were to hide inside its purple mantle a generous jigger of scotch. I suppose he felt that gin might suspiciously lighten the color of the concoction, but I cannot imagine a worse mixture. I never tasted it but Nat, who did, said that my imaginings didn't do justice to the nasty reality.

I am told that neither Ruth nor Heywood was much of a

drinker until after World War I when the passage of Prohibition made the cocktail a sort of toast to freedom, and this may
have been why Heywood showed signs of discomfort when at
about sixteen I started holding out a glass when the cocktail
shaker made its rounds. Ruth stuck to our old fiction that I was
a grown-up, and poured without a tremor, but Heywood
would ask pointless questions such as, "Are you sure you want
one?" which led to the inevitable answers, "If I didn't want one
I wouldn't be asking for it."

If I gave any thought to the whole business of their heavy
drinking, it was certainly not of the child's innocent horror that
is found in old temperance songs. I vaguely supposed that
everyone's parents took the sharp edges off the prospect of
another day with something more comforting than straight
orange juice. Although I didn't feel the need at sixteen, I did
discover a couple of years later that a brandy or sherry flip,
drinks in which the addition of a well-beaten egg gave the
illusion that one was actually breakfasting, seemed to start the
day with an extra sparkle. I was, however, pretty selective
about the mornings on which I did this and in the end proved
too repressed and cautious a personality to get high and happy
before I got sick to my stomach.

So repressed was I, indeed, that I passed through the years
of traditional adolescent rebellion with no more than a little
additional withdrawal.

I kept meticulous accounts of forgotten allowances—and the
havey-cavey nature of household accounts made the forgetting a fairly frequent business—and I noted such small un-
returned loans as occasionally I made to them but, and here
was the icy pleasure, I never presented my reckonings for
collection. New clothes were never requested, which meant
that I went through several winters with slick paper magazine
covers stuffed in my shoes as an eventually rather gummy
defense against rain-soaked pavements, while in college I made

a scarlet mackinaw into a kind of defiant sartorial trademark because it was the only coat I had.

Of course, the trouble with this kind of rebellion is that it is so far underground that, like some guerilla band that starves to death in its mountain fastness, it goes totally unrecognized.

Once, and once only, when the exigencies of college romance made cash a vital matter—I had to buy a corsage—I telegraphed him for my overdue allowance. I got the check and he got the subject for a column about the improvidence of youth and its inability to keep its affairs in order. It was written in a jovial, friendly style that stoked the fires of my puritanical resentment like a bucket of gasoline. I sent him a note thanking him for the check and did not mention the column. A string of twelve straight winners—I telephoned in bets every day to my still active bookmaker's account—made it unnecessary for me to ask again that year, a fact that, of course, he didn't notice.

Enclosed in my own indissoluble capsule of self-concern, I was never aware of the extent of the fierce independence of my parents. They had tried to make me independent and in a way that they found painful had succeeded, but the extent of their need for each other I was incapable of understanding, just as I was incapable of understanding the resentment that dependent people feel against those on whom they depend. If you doubt it, think how angry babies get when their shouts for a diaper change go unheeded. Thrashing around in a crib, helpless as a turned-over turtle, they are the ultimate dependents and they don't forgive answers and solutions that are less then instant and complete.

The divorce, Heywood's well-advertised affairs, Ruth's hypercritical comments, Heywood's avoidance of all responsibilities except those to his job—all these things were weapons that could be wielded when dependency asked for something and didn't get it fast or fully enough. Since new needs came faster than answers to old needs, the intensity of the resentment grew until it frightened them and left them, a divorced couple, clinging together in a farmhouse, not reconciled but far from ready to try what lay beyond irreconcilable differences.

•   •

In the summer of 1934, while I was touring Europe on money given me by Ruth—characteristically Heywood waffled so long over whether this was a good idea that if she had not come up with the cash it would have been too late—she entered into her mysterious final illness. She died only a few weeks after I returned from my trip, after being rushed to a hospital over her feeble protests that she wanted to stay in Stamford.

The death was not quite real to me at first because I had been left behind with Mattie and Earl and had only heard about it over the telephone from Heywood. I remember the numbness of shock. I remember hanging up the phone in the little hall between kitchen and living room. I remember turning to tell Mattie, and I remember the silent drive into the city, but I held the doors against feeling. Feeling would mean looking at the causes of this mysterious illness, and I wasn't ready to hold up the weight of my guilt.

Able to write anytime anyplace, even in the ruins of his world, Heywood expressed his feelings in a column the day after Ruth's death.

My best friend died yesterday. I would not mention this but for the fact that Ruth Hale was a valiant fighter in an important cause. Concerning her major contention we were in almost complete disagreement for seventeen years. Out of a thousand debates I lost a thousand. Nobody ever defeated Miss Hale in an argument. The dispute was about feminism. We both agreed that in law and art and industry and anything else you can think of men and women should be equal. Ruth Hale thought that this could be brought about only through the organization of women along sex lines. I think that this equality will always be an inevitable and essential part of any thoroughgoing economic upheaval.

"Come on and be a radical," I used to say, but Miss Hale insisted on being a militant feminist—all this and nothing more and nothing less.

Deems Taylor once said to her: "Ruth, you have more capacity for emotion than anybody I ever knew. I wish I had it, because if I did I wouldn't waste it in such narrow channels."

Decidedly I am not unsympathetic with the Lucy Stone League, of which Miss Hale was the president and prime mover. I agree thoroughly with the slogan of the association, which runs "My name is the symbol of my identity and must not be lost." Men as well as women live by symbols. But when I spoke of the brotherhood of mankind, Miss Hale insisted on changing it into the sisterhood of womankind. "Mankind embraces womankind," I argued with due grammatical license. "It works just as well the other way," she responded, and the vigor of her drive moved me invariably to amend the familiar phrase and make it run "Are we mice or women?"

I could hardly deny the assertion that the Western world is still stacked in favor of the male sex. I refer less to existing gross inequalities in law than to the force of custom and tradition. This came closely home to both of us. When we met we were reporters, and I have never denied that Ruth Hale was the better newspaperman of the two. I think the things that held her back were biological. Brisbanes don't have babies.

• WHOSE LITTLE BOY ARE YOU? •

Vicarious expression was of no use to her. I may as well admit right off something which will soon be evident. A very considerable percentage of all newspaper columns, books and magazine articles which appeared under the name "Heywood Broun" were written by Ruth Hale. I mean, of course, the better columns. And even those which I felt I was writing on my own stemmed from her.

It was a curious collaboration, because Ruth Hale gave me out of the very best she had to equip me for the understanding of human problems. She gave this under protest, with many reservations, and a vast rancor. But she gave.

I understood this and will always understand the bitterness of the person who projects himself through another even if that one is close. Of course, in regard to a few minor points I felt that I was standing on my own feet. Miss Hale could never quite convince me that she could keep the boxscore of a baseball game more accurately than I could. What she could not realize was the fact that she demonstrated to me, at any rate, the kind of equality which inches up to a decided superiority. Since it is true that very many of the ideas for which I seem to be sponsor are really hers, in the last analysis I am the utterly dependent person.

She was not my severest critic. Her tolerance was broad to the mass of mediocre stuff the newspaper hack is bound to produce in seventeen years. Nobody else, I suppose, ever gave me such warm support and approbation for those days when I did my best. She made me feel ashamed when I faltered, and I suppose that for seventeen years practically every word I wrote was set down with the feeling that Ruth Hale was looking over my shoulder.

It would be a desperately lonely world if I did not feel

that personality is of such tough fiber that in some manner it must survive and does survive. I still feel that she
is looking over my shoulder.

Even here where the pain is so obvious that it seems to come
chattering out of the typewriter keys, Heywood couldn't help
trying to mask it, as he masked all his emotions, with little
whimsies about mice and box scores, but the fear is as clear as
the pain. The hand is gone and the abyss is deep and very rocky
at the bottom.

"In the last analysis I am the utterly dependent person," he
writes, and I think back to Frank Adams' light-hearted joke at
the wedding about the clinging oak and the sturdy vine. In
everything except his social views about the world Heywood
was timid. Physically, sexually, intellectually—the list is as
long as the list that Alvan Barach eventually gave me of Heywood's phobias, a list that made him call his former patient a
"pantophobe," or one almost universally phobic.

Ruth could not allay all those fears, but with her determination she could help him fight them and remind him that whatever the cost he had a larger fight on his hands that would need
his attention every day, the forwarding of his beliefs.

She didn't, as he wrote in the column about her, share many
of them. They did not differ solely on the issue of feminism.
The really big gap was on a really big issue, her absolute and
occasionally antisocial individualism—"If I want to build a
hideous and possibly obscene hundred-foot tower on my
property," she once said to me in a discussion of the merits of
zoning, "I'd like to see anyone try to stop me"—and his belief,
expressed both politically and at last religiously, that it is in
voluntarily formed ranks that we will triumph. They argued
endlessly about this but in the argument, in the interplay, she
was for a time pulled out of the emptiness that is the ambience
of individualism, the emptiness that was as diagramless as the
crossword puzzles that dotted it.

• WHOSE LITTLE BOY ARE YOU? •

They were both aware that in all the arts her taste was sharper and more informed than his. Basically, he liked boom-boom music, like the Wagner to which he jogged, sentimental books, well-written enough to hide their tinkly message, and his own pictures.

The statement made by him and many others, including me, that she wrote much of what was published under his name applies, I think, pretty much to critical pieces.

They did not agree enough politically for Ruth comfortably to ghost his work. All these essays have a rhythm of carefully timed short sentences that eventually create a wonderful kind of martial march step of their own. It was an evangelical style, far removed from Ruth's mandarin approach to writing. Still, as he admitted, she was always looking over his shoulder.

Of course, in this literary dependency, for all that she might exult over the strength of her influence, she had to be angry —she who proclaimed the slogan, "My name is the symbol, my identity which must not be lost"—ever losing it in the basic newspaper prerogative, the byline.

To have Heywood praised for what she had in large part done was an exhausting irritation, and it's still unclear why, except for a couple of theatrical press agent jobs and an unsuccessful stage adaptation of Elinor Wylie's novel, *The Venetian Glass Nephew*, she remained so professionally inactive after her marriage and after the divorce which was to restart all the creative machinery.

I sometimes wonder whether she envied her mother-in-law, Mrs. Heywood Cox Broun. It is true that Mrs. Broun proudly wore all the badges of servitude that feminists despise, and it's true that she came at last to indulge her husband in the belief that he was in charge of things, but I never met anyone more serenely independent. The only decision I knew her to share was to let Cousin Helen have a vote on the matter of whether it was close enough to lunchtime to permit ladies to drink.

Cousin Helen always seemed to vote for a surprisingly early hour like 11:30 A.M., which is perhaps why, when I would arrive at a little after noon for a chat and a meal, I would find the living room redolent of rum and blue with the smoke of the powerful Puerto Rican cigarettes they both favored. These brown-paper-wrapped ministogies gave off coils of heavy smoke that had to be beaten with a fan to make them change their shape. Being ladies they showed no effect in slurred speech from the smooth, sweet, powerful drinks that were made from my grandmother's special recipe, but I always limited myself to one lest I say or do something that a gentleman shouldn't say or do.

Although a product of the Victorian age, Henrietta Brosé had just the sort of upbringing that Ruth would have liked. Henrietta's mother died when the girl was very young, and the child took over the running of the household. At the age of twelve she presided over a staff of servants in Germany where business had taken her father, and served as hostess at formal dinners. I never heard that her father ever questioned her judgment, but I'm sure that if he did, it was not something he repeated. As the trolley motorman was later to find out, Henrietta could make you wish you hadn't crossed her.

The independence that Ruth kept looking for on the long journey from Rogersville was handed by chance to Heywood's mother along with the household account books.

She and Ruth never became friends but they came after awhile to a kind of understanding, Mrs. Broun respecting Ruth for the relentlessness of her battle against her own vulnerability, and Ruth admiring the old lady for being so splendidly invulnerable.

His mother had passed on some of her toughness to Heywood, enough so that with all his phobias baying at his heels he could stop and do a good deal more than his share to change a world for which his hopes, despite his fears, were romantically high, but she could not give him that most useful gift, certainty.

In the obituary column he confessed his debt to Ruth and admitted his need for her, but the man who wrote so eloquently had nothing further to say and never discussed her with me thereafter. At her own wish she was cremated, and because she had not wanted one, there was no sort of memorial service. One day she was there and the next day she was gone.

Some part of Heywood seemed to have gone with her, and I saw very quickly from physical signs that he was close to a breakdown. He did not drink any more than usual, but he slept a lot less and for the first time he began to look like a man who drank too much. His hands shook and he had the beginnings of a red nose.

He would sometimes summon me down from school in Riverdale for an evening of rather forced fun, but shyly aware that we weren't the best of companions, he saw to it that I had theater tickets every weekend so that I could take some friend from school who might better distract me than he, who felt as lost as I did.

I tried to drop my politely distant pose but discovered as Max Beerbohm's "Happy Hypocrite" had done that the mask once put on begins to shape the face beneath, so that my efforts at intimacy were as awkward as his. We were like a pair of schoolboys thrown together by a rooming chart who were not at all sure they were going to like each other but were making the best of things.

Talking about racing, politics, and the twists of comic-strip plots (this last we did rather guiltily because Ruth had always discouraged such talk, often with suggestions of more elevating reading), we whiled away a great many hours in a kind of club man's intimacy, that pleasure one takes in an informed chat with someone whose life and character outside the comfortable rooms of the club is not to be asked out.

After a first semester during which I saw thirty-three plays, in addition accompanying Heywood to far more than thirty-three restaurants and bars, my spring vacation arrived and Heywood took me to Miami with him. Here we got up just in time to go to the horse races in the afternoon where I breakfasted on the milder of the two flips, sherry, in order to keep my mind clear for handicapping. After the races we went to dinner and then to the dog track after which we sampled assorted night spots until it was time to get a good night's sleep before post time at Tropical Park.

After a few days of this and a bad run of luck at both tracks, I was broke. Knowing Heywood's iron rule about paying my losses without advances on the allowances, I was getting ready to announce that my afternoons would be spent by the swimming pool and my evenings with a book. At this point I received a five-dollar check forwarded from New York (I had gone back into a ten-share position in General Electric and this was the quarterly dividend), and, reprieved, went to the greyhound track with Heywood where by calling for the wrong numbers at the daily double window I won a large sum that was augmented by a string of fortunate choices that went on all through the next day.

Near the end of the vacation Heywood suggested that I skip a few days of school since the tide of fortune seemed to be running well. Since it was rare for him to come right out and beg for my company (I knew he knew too much about luck for any of that tide-of-fortune stuff to have any meaning), I was very much moved, but I had to explain that Horace Mann looked with strong disfavor at absence on top of vacation and passed out failing grades for every missed class to prove the vigor of its disapproval.

Heywood said he would give me a letter saying that he had had influenza and had kept me with him so that I might take care of him. I thought this pretty unconvincing but I didn't

think the school would give the lie to a distinguished old grad
so I stayed, had a good time, and confidently presented the
letter to a surprisingly chilly school proctor who suggested that
I look at the bulletin board. Pinned to it was a column by
Heywood in which he wrote that he could not keep up with
the pace of youth. In proof of this he adduced the behavior of
his energetic son who had several times suggested that bed be
skipped altogether so that the dawn workout at the track could
be seen, to be followed by a hearty breakfast of ham and eggs
and a swim (he at least left out the sherry flips). Nothing was
said about influenza. The proctor read the letter, then looked
at me with the expression of someone lifting a rock to find a
deformed albino tarantula (I actually did that once in Arizona
so I know what one looked like).

I was permitted to return to my classes without penalty, but
it seemed to me from expressions on faculty faces that it was
not a good time for me to be guilty of any small infractions of
discipline.

I complained to Heywood about the column but he, having
received a good word or two about it from readers, just laughed
and said that nobody would take it seriously. The fact that I
did didn't seem to count.

I was annoyed with Heywood for not showing proper solici-
tude for my interests, but in the atmosphere of intimate es-
trangement that marked our relationship at the time, I was
capable of being just as mad at him for having too much
concern for my interests.

When the Newspaper Guild was conducting a strike against
the Newark *Ledger,* I was promised that I would be allowed one
evening to be a picket. I was filled with romantic "Waiting-for-
Lefty" notions and I saw myself, fatally wounded by a policeman's bullet, husking out some soon-to-be-immortal labor
slogan just before the gush of bright blood from the corner of
my mouth signaled the end of the scene and my tragically short

life. Perhaps a folk song would immortalize me, a kind of prep school Joe Hill who would be remembered as long as fighters for a better world got together to harmonize.

It was raining when we arrived at strike headquarters and picketing, either by judicial fiat or because of the weather, was limited to a single placard waver in front of the main entrance to the *Ledger* building. When it was my turn I was hung about with sandwich boards, given a defiant sign nailed to a stick, and taken to my post by Heywood.

When we arrived there the policeman on duty came to attention, *saluted* Heywood, and gave me a friendly smile that suggested that it would take a good deal of provocation to get him to shoot me.

Heywood then made it worse. "This is my boy, Harrigan," he said, "Take good care of him."

I smile now, and as a father understand his careful launching of my career as a strike activist, but at the time I felt very young and humiliated. The heroism of the evening was all Heywood's. When the sports editor of the paper came out of the building, flanked by a couple of men who looked like bodyguards, Heywood, who had been watching from a window, perhaps to see if I stepped in puddles and got my feet wet, came bursting out, shouldered the guards aside, and said boldly, "I want to talk to you." It was a pretty nervy performance for a man afraid of crowds, cars, and elevators. The editor and Heywood went off to drink together and become friends, although no minds were changed, while I refused to get friendly with Harrigan and did get my feet wet.

It wasn't long after this demonstration of physical courage (the men really were bodyguards) that Heywood had a chance to display moral courage at a level that made me more ashamed than ever that I dared to resent him in any way—without lessening my resentment.

William Randolph Hearst had decided to add "It Seems to

Me" to the collection of columns in his papers, and he was a hard man to resist. Few people now remember what power he possessed or seemed to possess, and in a world with bogeymen to spare it's equally hard to remember how much right-wing support and left-wing opposition coalesced around the single figure of the chief, W.R., the man who always got what he wanted whether it was the Spanish American War or another writer for that stable of opinion molders that was headed by Arthur Brisbane, the highest-paid newspaperman in America.

Hearst's emissaries had not offered Heywood Brisbane's figure but the projected salary was much more than Scripps-Howard was paying and with it came the precious premise of editorial freedom, something he wasn't getting from a syndicate that omitted some columns and cut others to the point of incomprehensibility.

Joe Connolly, head of Hearst's King Features, was constantly on the phone with flattery and financial inducement until Heywood decided on a surcease to be achieved by absence and took me along on another Caribbean cruise.

On the cruise we did a lot of fishing and instead of the needled beer I had gotten in my early years of barhopping with him, I shared champagne with him every night. It appears that Connolly had instructed the wine steward of the *Lafayette* that we were to have a bottle with each of our dinners. Our host at a distance specified the brand and vintage year, both beyond criticism, but not, according to the sommelier, subject to change. I know it sounds decadent to say that one can get tired of champagne, but as two weeks of caviar might make one feel wistful about pimento cheese spread, so the identical bottles began to have not so much a festive look as the appearance of a mechanical prescription for frolic that you wished would run out.

After a week Heywood had the wonderful idea of mixing our regal treat with varying amounts of the vin ordinaire, red and white, that stood like salt and pepper shakers on every dining room table of a French ship. What the waiters thought I'd rather not guess, but variety, that spice of life, returned in drinks that tasted like everything from sparkling burgundy to a wedding punch made from a half-forgotten recipe.

The waiters could not have been any more surprised than the fishing captains Heywood interviewed at our ports of call. He would always ask whether they knew where to find sailfish, that game monster that gives hours of fighting fun to the real sportsman. When the captains invariably replied that they knew just the cove, Heywood would ask them to stay away from such places.

"I want plenty to eat and drink on the boat," he would tell them, "and I want to catch small fish."

Equipped with tackle designed to keep Leviathan on the hook, we flicked overmatched punies onto the deck of the boat while eating sandwiches, drinking beer, and continuing our discussions of politics, horse racing, and whether Dynamite Dunn could cross over from the pages of the *World Telegram* and beat Joe Palooka in the *Mirror* for the heavywight title.

The importunities of the Hearst organization continued after we returned from the cruise and the big clincher was supposed to be a dinner with Brisbane in which all the advantages of the deal would be laid out while the rich fruitiness of liqueurs danced with the flicker of firelight in the great man's leather-upholstered library.

While Brisbane was refilling the glasses with the right stuff and explaining how best to invest the big bonus that was the sweetener for the deal, Heywood noticed a steel-engraved portrait of a fierce-looking man who was scowling down at all this easy living from a spot over the mantelpiece.

"That's a handsome head," said Heywood. "Who is he?"

"That's my father, Albert Brisbane," was the answer. "He used to pay to get on the front pages of the New York papers.

He had them put on a headline that said 'This space bought by Albert Brisbane,' and then he'd use it to lambast the trusts, the banks, the railroads, and the government."

There was a reflective pause while the fire crackled encouragingly and the expensive furniture gave little luxurious whispers when the sitters shifted, and then Brisbane, looking down into his snifter, murmured in a voice just loud enough for his companion to hear, "You can bet your life he wasn't working for Hearst."

Heywood told the story to his intimates and always gave it as the reason why he eventually turned down the Hearst offer, but I think the real answer lay in the absence of the other half of the two-headed, one-hearted entity called Heywood Broun and Ruth Hale.

In a head-on fight Heywood was always very tough but soft words sometimes sapped him, as did his own self-doubt. "I was promised," he told me, "that my copy wouldn't be censored by anybody, but every word of opinion that goes into his papers is telegraphed to a machine wherever he is, and he reads it. How do I know I wouldn't censor myself? You know the kind of thing—seeing him in your mind's eye, frowning at something really good you've written, and then trying to choose a less cutting phrase, something that gets the point across without making him frown. That kind of thing is worse than the cuts you can holler about."

"I still feel," he had written, "that she is looking over my shoulder."

If Ruth had been there she could have pointed him at Hearst and fired him like a cannon. In the presence of Hearst I'm sure she could have made even the chief's hands feel like big red balloons. When they were together Ruth was conscience and Heywood was the voice of conscience.

Heywood once told an interviewer about an occasion when his very small son showed him a newspaper picture of a very large lion and asked if he would be afraid of it. Ritually Heywood said no he wouldn't and I am supposed to have shouted, "Yes you would, too"—and then, seeking an ultimate example, added, "Why even Ruth would be afraid of him."

Alone he was fearful that charming weekends at Hearst's San Simeon dream palace might dull the edges of his writing —unless, of course, he heard behind him the steel-backed voice that used to say, "You can do better than that," a voice that had faded into a phantom whisper warning him that Brisbane's advice had been sound. He took the advice, and I, visiting San Simeon years later as a television correspondent, hearing the coil of visitors ask again and again "Is that real gold?" wanted very much to tell Heywood how proud I was that his name wasn't in the visitors' book.

I thought then, too, of the strange power of a woman who collapsed into tears at a boy's criticism of a hair arrangement but who could raise an eyebrow and level a castle.

Heywood told a good many people about Brisbane's whisper, and gave it as his decisive reason for refusing the offer. Ruth's whisper is just my supposition, but it's a supposition based on how many times it seems that she has whispered rather sternly to me.

Nobility as a word describing behavior is uncomfortable these days, linked with masochism, rigidity, and impracticality. It is a cold sounding word, unsparing and cruel, as well as elitist and arrogant.

"You never know what a gentleman is," wrote Scott Fitzgerald, "until you cease to be one."

There are not, as in the comfortable gardens of pragmatism, any qualifying adjectives here. One is not fairly noble or pretty much a gentlemen. Judgment is continuous, unsparing, and unforgiving, and I'm sure that Ruth and Heywood would have had a much better time if they had believed in the hedonism that as social rebels they so assiduously espoused in the days when you never knew what freedom was until you experienced it.

When even for a moment at San Simeon I felt a passing regret that Heywood's nobility had kept me from a glorious day or two when, surrounded by movie starlets, I could have galloped on vine-roofed bridle paths, grabbing at grapes on the run, a whole wind of whispers told me I should be ashamed of myself, and after a rebellious moment I was.

• •

Praise is very hard to win in the world of perfectionist assessment, and for Heywood the cheerful, uncomplicated admiration he got as part of his second marriage was particularly welcome as the creaks of middle age became the voices of his phobias and the weariness of work seemed to make it harder to keep their ring from closing and crushing.

I thought remarriage was just the thing for him, but for a variety of reasons, all of which seemed rational at the time, I didn't tell him so. Indeed, I handled the business as I had been trained to, which meant as handsomely as I had managed the affair of where I was to live.

As usual when Heywood had something momentous to tell me, he took me to a nightclub, where a good surround of strangers made heart-to-heart talks seem more like idle exchanges. "I'm thinking of getting married again," he said after a number of false starts about important changes had trailed off into cigarette lightings. "It's Connie."

A protest might have been difficult but would at least have been an indication of my emotional involvement, and a handshake and a hug would have been hoped-for encouragement. What he got was the tolerant smile of someone agreeing to a change of golf dates and the comment that it was polite of him to tell me what was in fact none of my business. I congratulated him with the casual goodwill of an office colleague hearing the news. For once he let his hurt show and protested with a twisty sort of smile that of course it was my business. Wasn't I after all a part of the family of which Connie was about to become a member?

This didn't seem to me up to the standards of freedom that had been part of the creed I took in with my bottles and baby food, part of the agreement that had set up the federation of states on Eighty-fifth Street.

I liked Connie, I said patiently, and thought that the marriage would be good for him (like many public persons he had more cronies than friends and I had been shocked at the random restless nature of his recent social life, but these thoughts I kept to myself). I was disappointed, however, I went on, that he would think me the kind of burdensome and incomplete person who would feel any right to interfere with his freedom. I was, after all, almost nineteen and would soon be going off to college and then perhaps to graduate school, which meant that my place in his life would be small, and I certainly had no wicked-stepmother feelings about Connie. I had accepted the divorce calmly as something concerning the freedom of Ruth and Heywood (this was the only lie in my performance) and I could therefore be calm about a much more hopeful happening, his remarriage. I didn't go so far as to ask what their silver pattern was going to be in my parody of second cousin receiving news of a marriage of relatives at the edge of his circle, but my knife was long enough and sharp enough as it was, and I cannot be surprised at the coolness Nat Benchley detected a year or two later. I wasn't surprised when I wasn't invited to the wedding, but I don't remember the reason given as to why I wasn't.

I am a great believer in Dr. Willard Gaylin's dictum, "We are what we seem to be," which is, after all, just a variant on Wilde's "A gentlemen is never unintentionally rude," and I have many times blamed myself for my appalling behavior on hearing about Heywood's plans, but my God, it was the natural outcome of an upbringing that could only be justified—and its practitioners forgiven—if one acted according to its principles.

At the time, when those who heard about my behavior rebuked me, I was bewildered and said I thought Heywood would be glad that he didn't have to worry about me.

On the other hand when Annie Riley Hale, her ripsaw teeth undulled by the years, asked me after the wedding how I liked the funeral-baked meats being used for the wedding feast, I turned on her with a speech I wish Heywood could have heard. I wondered why she ignored the fact that her daughter had divorced him, and I went on with rising vigor into confused praise of marriage in general hampered by, but not deterred by, a lack of knowledge, then became more sensible and more detailed in my praise of the marriage of Connie and Heywood. I said I thought it would be the salvation of Heywood and that if it had not happened the funeral-baked meats might well have been in good enough shape to be used for another funeral, his, and that I wished never to speak to her again.

I didn't, in fact, speak to her for four years and then didn't speak to my uncle Richard for another year because he, gentle and loving person that he was, could not bear his mother's unhappiness about the breach and invited me to dinner without telling me that she would be there. The best I can say for myself is that I was affable, if distant. When Mrs. Hale left at the end of the evening I gave her the kiss she demanded, and I waited until she was safely down the stairs before I told my uncle how angry I was at the deception. That anger soon cooled because I could not long be mad at this man whose sweetness was a striking contrast to the rest of the family that I knew, and apparently an inheritance from that dim Papa who had too many horses for the size of his farm and not enough nerve to climb on one of them and ride away from Rogersville.

My calm at Heywood's wedding announcement was made easier by the fact that I had long been expecting it.

He had met Connie in 1931 at the rehearsals of his essay in theatrical production, *Shoot the Works.* He put it on with the laudable idea of lessening unemployment in the theater and with the self-serving idea of getting back on the stage, something he had been longing for ever since the days when the Algonquin crowd had put on a couple of one-night revues to the enthusiasm of their friends and the dismay of their fellow critics. Out of that original group Bob Benchley became a successful movie actor, Alec Woollcott had some success playing stylishly disagreeable versions of himself, and Heywood had twelve weeks of expensive fun at the George M. Cohan Theatre.

Shoot the Works was a loosely organized collection of borrowed songs and sketches. The principal and almost only piece of stage furniture was a big bed under which, at one time, five actors, among them Heywood, were hiding.

The costumes were mostly brought from home although the discovery of a bunch of big Mexican straw hats left in the cellar by some long forgotten Shubert effort at profitable Latin gaiety led to the hasty concoction of an "Olé!" number. Some of the girls complained that insects, nesting in the hats, were disturbed by stamping feet and bongo drumming to the extent of stinging the ankles circling the broad brims.

The show varied a good deal from night to night as various friends of Heywood's dropped in and performed for a few nights. The Marx Brothers arrived in town and, hearing that Broun had put on a show subtitled "For Unemployed Actors," announced that they qualified that week and added themselves to the cast.

Helen Morgan gave several nights of song and Irving Berlin contributed a number for which he hadn't yet found a place. Other performers just dropped in unannounced after dinner and the necessarily ramshackle running order would be adjusted to accommodate them.

One sketch that was dropped over the producer-costar's protests was a playlet by Heywood called *Death Says It Isn't So.* This was a very effective little scene in which MacNamara in a loud checked coat played a jolly reaper with a fine fund of tricks and jokes while the veteran comedian Percy Helton was a dying stagehand full of old-fashioned ideas about the grimness of death's character. He eventually dies laughing at something Mac whispers in his ear.

No one laughed for about forty minutes after Helton's laughter-turned-coughing faded along with the lights, and the comedians who had to work through that stretch complained until their kind-hearted boss trimmed it out of the show.

It is one of the few things I remember from the production, which I saw only on its steaming hot opening night, but I am probably the only living human being who can sing all the words of "I'm Just a Doorstep Baby" ("People point at me with scorn, why don't they seem to realize that I didn't ask to be born?") which I learned from Heywood during the many mobile songfests in the car.

Connie, her husband having died shortly before the birth of a daughter, Patricia, had seen her widow's portion disappear in the crash of 1929 and had moved in with her family in Yonkers and returned to the stage as a means of helping keep things afloat.

In old-time musicals the wistfully pretty heroine had a lively snub-nosed friend who cheered her up when the moon of romance went behind the clouds, did a funny song with the comic friend of the handsome hero, and paired off with the friend at the curtain calls as the moon of romance came up to full wattage and everybody sang a rousing reprise of the better songs.

The female friend figure was called the soubrette and was,

according to the *Oxford Dictionary* definition, "usually one of a pert, coquettish, or intriguing character."

Connie was living proof that the most theatrical of stage conventions are the ones most closely based on reality. She was the soubrette in excelsis right down to the bobbed dark hair and the ever-present bright smile. She closely resembled Zelma O'Neale and Patsy Kelly, the reigning soubrettes of that day, and unrehearsed, talked all day in the style she practiced from 8:40 to 11:15.

She consoled Heywood for the show's relative lack of success—from opening night to final curtain *Shoot the Works* cost Heywood $7,500, the amount usually spent on the mailing for a preproduction press party today, but they were 1931 dollars, hard to come by, and proof, as they drained away, that Heywood's dream of theatrical eminence was about to dissolve— and I imagine that their affair began during or shortly after the closing of the show.

I say imagine because Ruth and Heywood, despite all their constant talk about sexual freedom, and their not so constant practice of its privileges, were usually, as far as I was concerned, as discreet as those Edwardians who listened for the dawn bell rung in country houses as a signal that they should tiptoe back to their own rooms.

I still remember my shock when a girl turned her head on a pillow and said "I guess this is sort of a tradition. I suppose you know that your mother had an affair with my father."

I pretended to the knowledge even as I wondered worriedly if incest might be involved, an idea I abandoned when I remembered that this politically powerful lover had gotten Ruth a low license plate number, a presumed dating of the liaison, when I was twelve years old.

After the divorce Heywood and Connie were naturally much more open about seeing each other and although this upset Ruth a good deal, she had put herself in a position where she could not complain to anyone except Mattie, with whom her relationship was so loving and so absolute that everything was understood and everything forgiven.

It would take too long to catalogue all the differences between Ruth and Connie, but perhaps they are best summed up in the fact that Ruth thought "Live and let live" was the motto of the damned and Connie thought it was the golden rule.

As one of the four daughters of a poor Italian laborer, Maria Incoronata Fruscella (not much of a stage name) had gone from a confined childhood to the uncertain gaieties of theatrical life to the romantic peak of marriage to a star, the dancer Johnny Dooley, a headliner himself and brother of the headliner Rae Dooley, a great comedienne. Dooley's death and the subsequent return to square one I never heard much about.

"Nobody wants to hear your sad stories," she would chirp. "You've got to keep dancing," and with a determined if narrow philosophy of taking things as they came and seeing what could be made of them, she—like the antique Orphan Annie of the radio series who "Always has a cheery word handy"— kept dancing, or at least smiling, through a second brief marriage, and a second widowhood, a rather dull one punctuated by afternoons of bridge and a lot of television.

If Ruth had set out to improve Heywood, Connie set out to make him happy, and both were good at what they did. Heywood, because of the daunting reserve that lay behind his anxious twinkles, had not had a friendly nickname since the Horace Mann days when he was called "Rube" possibly because he was big and soft-spoken like the farmer heroes of contemporary melodrama.

Connie started calling him "Commander." It was flattering, only endearingly silly, and a reassuring name for one who had defensively worn a fedora with an officer's uniform.

She made an effort at smartening his clothes, and so that they should not look like wrinkled sausage casings, had a good try at getting him to lose weight, one aid to which was to be a diminution of his drinking. It was during this period that the "Woodie, if you'd just bring me a grape juice" code was invented. I often wondered if I weren't doing something akin to Heywood's trick of smuggling booze to Dorothy Parker in the hospital. (Alvan Barach, medical officer to the Algonquin Army, had immured Mrs. Parker in a controlled environment in which, on a diet of fruit juice and custard, she was to get dried out in prospect of a new life. It seemed, however, that the days on which she appeared to have had her fruit juice mysteriously and deleteriously augmented coincided with the days of Mr. Broun's visits and he was banned from her room. It was one of the few discreditable things I had known him to do and it troubled me to be in emulation of it.) Still, I decided that if I disobeyed or balked I would only widen the gap that had been growing between Heywood and me since I disavowed an interest in his remarriage.

Whatever my motives in that act, I had ignored the simple fact that without me and Mattie around he would be free of ties to the old life and therefore more comfortable in the new.

Mattie had solved half his problem by discreetly departing for beauticians' school shortly before the wedding, aware, as sadly we all were, that tact demanded the move.

Although he became neither a teetotaler nor a top-to-toe fashion plate, Heywood seemed to enjoy being fussed over, but through friends I heard that he suspected me of disapproval, of hiding behind my grave politeness a strong sense that the new Heywood, a sort of slovenly country squire much given to woodchopping and health kicks, was smaller in more than waist measurements.

His attitude toward me became as fitful as the fitness program that swung between lashings of scotch and grape juice, and sessions of suffering in his rubber sweat suit.

He pleaded with me to take the *Nutmeg* job, and gave me lots of space to fill, took a large and informed interest in my choice of college, and in many other overt ways did a good job of playing the "concerned Dad."

"If you know absolutely what you want to do with your life in college, go to the biggest and best place where you can do it," he told me. "Remember that that will be the only thing you can do. In a big school year you can be a scholar, a football player, or the editor of the college paper, but not any two of them. The competition is too tough. If you don't know what you want to do, and you certainly don't seem to, go to some small school where owing to the small number of students everybody does several things."

He picked a college, Swarthmore, and I picked a college, Wesleyan, and in the end I went to Swarthmore because it didn't ask me, as Wesleyan did, to fill out a long and rather complex questionnaire.

As in the matter of gambling he had distilled out of his failure, in this case, his lost feeling at Harvard and his four-year flop there, some richly practical advice.

On the other hand he took me at my word about my independence and frequently embarked on long trips without telling me, so that when on weekends I turned up at the hotel that had replaced the apartment as his city pied à terre, I would be told by a clerk that he had left no messages or forwarding address. Often broke on these occasions, I would have to scare up a school friend with some spare space and parents willing to lend me a little something until times got better.

Wall-building is an addictive business and I took to disappearing for occasional stretches of a week or so, in order that I could answer casually couched but anxious questions with answers so opaque that any sophisticated hearer would have to assume I had been spending most of my hours in what used to be called "dens of vice." The fact that I had done nothing more than see three baseball games, a couple of Two-for-One shows at the Paramount, and spend a day with some old stuffed friends in the Museum of Natural History was my secret.

I don't really suppose the dens-of-vice theory was widely held, however, since somewhere in this stretch Jimmy Cannon, then a young crime reporter, was asked by Heywood to take me to a clean respectable whorehouse as a means of lessening my timidity with girls, and, if I seemed to enjoy the experience, allaying Heywood's fears that I might be homosexual.

Cannon, who was and remained an admirer of Heywood's, declined this office and I was left, like a great many prep school boys of the thirties, to a late start that may have been all the more delightful for the delay.

I thought of this during the so-called psychiatric examination for potential draftees on Governor's Island. Sitting next to the thin wall I heard several men being asked the question "Do you get laid regular?" to which they replied with a possibly truthful "Yes."

When the doctor read the extent of my education off the card I carried, he adjusted his vocabulary and asked "Normal sexual interest in women?" the only form of the question to which I could say "Yes."

One of the ways in which the family breach was symbolized was the abandonment of the family holiday dinner. Grandmother Broun was still good for a couple of rubbers of bridge after the revivifying effects of a couple of glasses of rum, but she was not able any more to organize big dinners, and after the death of Cousin Helen, no one wanted to preside, so the family fragmented into many subunits, one of which was, all-by-myself, me.

Heywood and Connie were invited each year to spend Thanksgiving with Averell Harriman, who either did not know of my existence or, less likely, knew of it and deplored it. In any case I was on my own for this great family holiday and spent it at such varied sites as the Haverford Township-Upper Darby High School football game, at the movies, or with those same friends who came up with the cost and the loans on weekends.

I didn't go home for my birthday or anyone else's, and Christmases were often spent comfortably if somewhat emptily in warm-weather resorts where unfilled boxes surrounded the artificial tree in the lobby. In my room I would get out the Gideon Bible and read, as I always had, St. Luke's account of the Nativity, feeling as guilty as square boys did about forbidden dime novels.

Once, Heywood and I went on a Caribbean cruise for Christmas and as midnight approached on the twenty-fourth we crept up to the front of the ship and, sitting beside a lifeboat like a couple of stowaways catching some air, sang carols in low embarrassed voices.

Another time, again in the years between Ruth's death and his remarriage, he took me to New Orleans, then the gambling capital of the country, Las Vegas being no more than a village.

Christmas at the racetrack was pleasant enough with more winners, if I remember rightly, than we had on the other days of our stay, but New Year's Eve was disorganized to the point that Heywood went off to play the wheel and I went to the movies and watched big glittering cardboard bells swing across the screen at midnight with the modest promise that next year would have to be better than one that ended in a double feature in a strange town.

I was grateful that Connie always made an honest effort to find something I really wanted on gift-giving occasions, and was at last consciously put out with Heywood when he, in Texas, forgot to call me on that most symbolic of birthdays, my twenty-first. Anger lasted about ten seconds before, without consciously thinking I might be giving him diphtheria, I began to bank my fires with smothering shovelfuls of laughter as I made the incident into a funny story for my college friends. Sturdily and unfortunately they organized a whole party in the soda-fountain section of the local drugstore, complete with a candle-bearing cupcake. For once I did what a normal person would do in these circumstances, and cried. Perhaps my friends were tired of my funny stories.

The next day, of course, Heywood called and beginning with the unfortunate sentence, "Did I forget your birthday?", proceeded to an extensive apology that I received with the warmth of a collection agency getting a promise instead of a check.

Heywood and I were about at the peak of our alienation on the occasion of a party for Mrs. Roosevelt, which may be why he forgot to introduce me to her, an oversight she corrected in her firm and somewhat frightening way.

The ostensible reason for the party was that the author of the column "My Day" had joined the Newspaper Guild, making her the first member of a presidential family to hold a union card—other than a ceremonial one.

I think the real reason was that Heywood wanted to show off to his mother. As far as I know this was the only time Grandmother Broun came to Stamford, and as she was well along in her eighties and sadly crippled by arthritis, it must have taken some persuasion.

Helped from the limousine she was established in a large chair where she could see everything. Hearing everything was more doubtful. Irving had bought her a hearing aid but she refused to have it adjusted to her individual needs because she said she was likely to die at any moment and did not wish to put anyone to the expense of such a long-range project as a couple of tuning visits. She did not like people to shout at her, however, and when her keen vision revealed the red face and distended neck chords of the bellower she would say sharply that there was nothing the matter with her hearing, and, even when this was manifestly untrue, we all had to learn to project penetratingly but without visible effort, a trick I was to find useful in my later years in the theater.

The party was pretty full of Stamford literati, the celebrity quotient among them being very high, when the guest of honor arrived and instantly became the super celebrity. Deems Taylor, Gene Tunney, Faith Baldwin, Quentin Reynolds, and others worthy of the attentions of Walter Winchell, fell into attitudes of awe and tried to crowd around the new Guild member.

She sailed right through them and settled herself at my grandmother's side. She had been taught that upon entering a room full of people one began a conversation with the eldest person present and she had no difficulty in telling that the matriarch in lilac silk filled the bill. Certainly nobody else in the room had such telltale additional signs as a pearl choker, an ebony cane, and the obtrusive bulk of an old-fashioned hearing aid.

Anxious to get on with introductions, Heywood hung about the edges of their talk, but he had forgotten the second half of the rule which decrees that the chat with the senior guest must be of reasonable duration and not just a hurried "Hello-how's-your-health?". My grandmother had no trouble hearing Mrs. Roosevelt who might tend to flute a little on platforms but had for social purposes a voice that, not loud, could be heard over all the shrieks at a children's party. Of course, my grandmother was a Republican, but she knew one didn't discuss politics at this sort of gathering, and they got on wonderfully, extending the visit beyond the outmost bounds set by politeness.

When a perspiring host finally was able to get the attention of his famous guest, I had already made two trips to nearby houses in search of more ice and mixers. Later trips took me into town for peanuts, the afternoon papers, and several other things that had been forgotten in all the excitement of getting ready for the *great visit.*

As a result of all this scurrying I had been barely visible for most of the day, but there had been several chances to say, "And this is my son, Woodie," which had passed, unused.

I was in the pantry pouring something into something when a tall cloaked figure appeared in the doorway and said "Thank you so much for having me. I had a very good time."

Unaided she had figured out who the waiter in blue jeans was and, of course, when leaving, one says goodbye to all the family.

I took Heywood to task about the omission and he had the grace to be uncomfortable, but most bad feelings were washed away with the good news that Grandmother quite approved of Heywood's new friend who didn't seem radical at all.

In between the unhappy moments there were the convulsive grabs at the return to something of the mellow ease that breathed out of those early columns about a young father's enjoyment of his son. It was perhaps with some memory of Eighty-fifth Street New Year's liveliness that Heywood expressed dismay as the year 1939 approached and I announced my intention of going into New York City for the purpose of taking a girl on a round of night spots.

Surely, Heywood protested, it would be more fun if I brought the girl to Stamford for a good old-fashioned family celebration. This was followed by hints that a new year might be a good time to start a new and better relationship.

I was touched and had my own misty vision of the return of the golden-haired little ladler of punch who would now be privileged to drink the stuff as well as dispense it.

Somewhere between Heywood's impulse and its execution, the usual withdrawal of the exploratory turtle's head occurred and the party turned out to have, in addition to the girl and me, a middle-aged couple whose only grace as far as I could tell was a sound bridge game. They sat down to an evening of cards with Connie and Heywood while the girl and I spent a wretchedly aimless evening until, at midnight, play was suspended for the opening of a bottle of champagne and the expression of good wishes.

I couldn't believe that that nightmare evening was pre-planned as some sort of vengeful punishment of an unsatisfactory son, although a bruised ego will take center stage if it can't get anything else, but I could not believe either that the isolation and ennui of the young people went unremarked even if it was ignored.

I spent some fruitless time brooding about it in the weeks and months that followed, forgot it for a long stretch of years, remembered it when seeking for a yardstick to measure another dull evening, thinking this time that direct efforts seemed to be our most disastrous means of getting things done.

We seemed to do better by indirection as indicated by his peculiar campaign to get me to quit college at the end of sophomore year. The reward for this act was to be a post with the copyboy staff of *The New York Times.* He said he could, through connections, get me one of these coveted appointments that would lead to eventual elevation to reportorial status.

I had been thinking of quitting school, not because I had some fascinating alternative in mind but because of simple restlessness and the sting of association with a place where my first romance had foundered. Someplace else, something else, I speculated vaguely, but one thing I was sure of—I didn't want to be in the newspaper business.

"You can get your career started right away," said Heywood with the enthusiasm of one who had been marching with Hildy Johnson and Richard Harding Davis from his first "Beau Broadway" piece in a 1910 *Morning Telegram* to his final column in the New York *Post* almost thirty years later.

"I don't want to be a newspaper man," I said, "I want to be a teacher." This was a fugitive idea briefly held when I was engaged to the girl with whom I had agreed that life on faculty row would give us summers off for passion-packed trips.

"A teacher," said Heywood, pronouncing the profession as if it lay in the leaden company of night elevator operation and ledger posting. "What do you want to be a teacher for? That's a terrible job. Being a newspaperman is the most exciting thing in the world. You'll love it."

He scoffed at my idea that it was difficult for me to follow in his footsteps. Very soon all that would be forgotten and I would be accepted into the company of the best bunch of people in the world. I had only to say the word and he would be on the phone to the *Times*.

As for the value of college, he had some pretty good arguments there, too. Once college had taught you how to use a reference library intelligently, he claimed, it could do nothing more for you. The art of looking things up was more complex than it might first appear, but he could tell that I had mastered it and the wisdom of the world was therefore available to me. I didn't need two years of marking time in lecture halls. I needed a valuable two-year jump on my contemporaries who would just be getting started on emptying city room wastebaskets and taking coffee orders from the night copydesk while I was off to cover my first fire.

The upshot, after two or three weeks of wrangling, was a hardening of my ambition to teach, a return to college, and a discovery by me of the basic selfishness of Heywood's plot, a discovery that I shared with horrified friends.

"You see," I told them. "He had only one great failure in life, his inability, after four years, to get a college degree. I am a pretty good student and the odds are that I will get a good degree, perhaps even garnished with a Phi Beta Kappa key. It will be the first time I have defeated him and he doesn't like it."

In the intensity of his wish that I follow in his professional footsteps he even once let me actually be Heywood Broun.

• WHOSE LITTLE BOY ARE YOU? •

Ralph Ingersoll, getting together a dummy issue of the adless newspaper he was soon to publish under the name *PM*, asked Heywood to put together the sports pages. Heywood turned the job and its emolument over to me, and I wrote a sports column signed with the parental name and a large number of news stories, sharing this work with a friend, Ed O'Neill, a newspaperman I had met when he covered Swarthmore college events for a local paper. O'Neill and I then made up our work into a four-page tabloid day-in-sport and Heywood forwarded it to Ingersoll.

A couple of years later I was frozen with embarrassment when, after I had gone to work for *PM* in the fall of 1940, Ingersoll called me into his office for a *solemn moment.* It seems he had a special gift for me, something I hadn't seen, one of my father's last works and one which he, Ingersoll, felt was right up to Heywood's high standards. He then presented me with a copy of the dummy newspaper that included our sports pages.

It is a measure of my confusion and resentment that I felt no glow at the praise for my ghost work.

I was so sick of old newspapermen maundering on about the task that lay ahead for me that the solace of thinking of how Heywood would at last be pleased with me did nothing more than keep me from quitting.

Harold Ross put it succinctly when he said, "You write well, Woodie, but you don't like to write."

Nat Benchley told me I should have fainted with pleasure at receiving some of Ross' grudgingly doled approval, but I said I was only struck by the shrewdness of his judgment.

Full of learning, I pointed out that everyone had heard of the Oedipus complex but few knew of the Laius complex, named for Oedipus' father who, after hearing from an oracle that his son would be his doom, ordered a slave to pierce the boy's feet and leave him at the roadside. This newspaper business I said was a sort of ritual piercing of the feet. When I went to work on the *Times* there would be two people named Heywood Broun, neither of whom had been graduated from college, both of whom worked on newspapers, one of whom was a master of the journalist's art, and the other of whom went out for sandwiches. It is a pretty logical argument, leaving out all that dramatic stuff about my feet, and seems the kind of thing an insecure father might do to his son without any conscious knowledge of the hostility involved.

And yet I find this in the pages of *The Boy Grew Older*, his novel about a newspaperman raising his son, a book full of my childish doings.

"He at last lost his temper and shouted at the child "All right then, don't eat any spinach. I won't let you eat any spinach."

Pat [me] scowled and, reaching all the way across the table, helped himself to a large spoonful. "I'm eating spinach," he said, "I'm eating it right now."

The only thing of which Peter [Heywood] had a right to boast was that he did not allow any false pride to stand between him and the object which he sought. He was quick to seize his opportunity. Pat's seeming free will was harnessed to serve the predetermined purposes of an ego less powerful but more unscrupulous.

"Maybe you are eating a little spinach," said Peter, "but I guess you won't dare take any milk when I tell you not to."

Pat fell into the trap. "Look at me now, Peter, I'm drinking it all up."

Is my diploma, then, written in milk on a leaf of spinach? I was still thinking of our academic competition when I did achieve a Phi Beta Kappa key at my graduation. When asked

how I wished the key engraved I said, "I am, in most everything, Heywood Hale Broun so as not to be confused with the
famous one, but in the limited field of scholarship, I guess I'm
Heywood Broun so engrave the key without the Hale."

A couple of years later the key got lost in a laundry and since
it wasn't much use to an army sergeant, and I didn't seem likely
to become a lawyer, I forgot about it until urged long afterward
by my son to send for another. Without thinking much about
it I filled out an application with Heywood Hale Broun in block
letters and only later realized that the name business no longer
seemed to concern me.

I told my friends that I was at last, and high time too, grown-
up and finished with this endless and exhausting measurement
against the mighty figure of Heywood Broun.

I also told the story to a psychoanalyst friend at a party and
he put on one of those enigmatic smiles and said, "Look at it
another way, Woodie. Your father had just died and you,
fearful and lost, wanted to give him a palliatory gift. Since he
had not been graduated you gave him the gift of your key.
Later, irritated at your action, you succeeded in losing the key
and obliterating the gift, and much later and much more satisfyingly, you took the gift back entirely by getting a key with
your name on it."

I told him that was one of the most discouraging things I'd
ever heard and he broke into a real smile and said, "I haven't
any idea whether my version is true, but then you don't have
any idea whether your version is true."

It's hard to free associate footnotes but suddenly all this
writing of the word "key" carries me to the kind of linked
irrelevancy that appears in small type at the bottoms of pages.

It is a memory of Heywood and me at a breakfast table in
1930. I am telling him a dream I had had a couple of months
previously at school in Tucson. In it I am in my little dormitory
room and I hear coming down the hall one of the school serv-

ants. He is running and shouting angrily and he is going to kill me with a carving knife I somehow know he is carrying. He is crying out, "My keys! You have stolen my keys!"

Forgetting, if he never knew it, the dictum against glibness in psychiatric matters, Heywood smiled in a knowledgeable way and, since we were both adults, gave me an explanation that, even at the time, seemed to prove that we weren't both adults.

"The dream is quite clear," he said. "The keys are an obvious symbol of the genitals, the knife is also obvious, and the servant is me. You in the competition for the physical love of your mother have had subconscious thoughts that are forbidden by taboo, and guilty about them, arrange that I, your rival, shall punish you."

I don't remember what I replied but I do suddenly hear the old jazz song, "Who Stole the Lock?" and think that "glib" is sometimes just another way of saying "understandable," and am not surprised that we would like things to be understandable.

I would like to understand a dream I often have now about Heywood. We meet on a street corner, usually near the apartment on Fifty-eighth Street, the place where he was living when the divorce was announced. I express surprise that I have not seen him in years and years and with an uncomfortable shrug he says that he has been pretty busy but now has a new place where he hopes I will come and see him. The dream ends before he manages to give me either the address or the phone number. When I first wake up I often wonder muzzily why I didn't follow him home or why I so easily accepted the lame explanation about being busy. Since we make up our own dreams, I'm told, I wonder why I don't ask him to come and have a drink with me. Can I not manage a little shadow hospitality in the barroom of the unconscious? Or is it that I'm afraid we would somehow end up at something like that 1939 New

Year's Eve party, or end up going to the wrong bars and missing each other.

I remember, for instance, the occasion at a baseball training camp in 1948 when Moe Berg, the erstwhile scholarly baseball catcher who was also a lawyer licensed to practice before the United States Supreme Court, told me of the time he had accompanied Heywood to Washington to hear testimony in the Morris Watson Case, an important piece of litigation involving the Newspaper Guild.

Heywood had insisted, according to Moe, that they stop off in Philadelphia and take the local train to Swarthmore so Moe could meet Heywood's remarkable son, a polymath who would stagger even Moe, according to the proud father.

Unfortunately nobody bothered to call me to tell me of the forthcoming visit, and I was unfindable.

The story of the trip to Washington as I heard it from Heywood had only a glancing reference to the side trip and dealt largely with the irony that the testimony that day had been so nit-picking and boring that Heywood had given up and gone off to see the Washington Senators play baseball while Moe, veteran of fifteen years of baseball, stayed to savor the small points his colleagues were curving past the justices.

There is, I'm sure, at least a little common sense in dreams. We did much better at a distance, as exampled by Heywood's printing in his column a piece I had written for a college political magazine. He introduced it with words of praise (he found these things easier to write than to say) that, now that I've reread it, seem to be exceptionally generous. He even went so far as to save, out of the largely untended flow of his correspondence, the two or three letters of commendation that the reprint evoked. It was a reach across the gap, a kind of metaphorical giving of that phantom address and phone number in the dream.

As indirect as he, I endeavored in my turn to do something

that would indicate appreciation by trying to establish a reasonably easy relationship with Connie and her daughter Patricia, a bewildered nine-year-old who, having been told by her mother to be as noiseless and inconspicuous as possible in her new house, moved about like a shadow looking for the safety of a dark wall.

About the only visible emotion between us was that, for the first time since I wouldn't go bed in 1922, he lost his temper with me. The matter itself was trivial. We were to go to Saratoga, and as train time approached I urged that we had better get organized and under way. To my amazement he turned on me sharply and actually snarled that since I had my own car why didn't I set out by myself and leave the rest of them in peace. I was more stunned than hurt, and even more surprised when about five minutes later he came back into the room with an apology, a first since he hadn't apologized for whacking me toward the stairs in 1922.

In the course of twenty years I had certainly done enough irritating things to evoke a hundred blows and a thousand shouts of threatening or warning nature, and parents, of course, have an infinite capacity for arousing the rage of their children. Still, going back and forth through the disorderly files jammed into the attics of my brain, I find just the four red-tabbed pages indicating temporary loss of control, the one brief spanking from each of them, one bark about making a train, and my outburst at Ruth for who knows what frustration just before her diphtheria attack.

What made us such a trio of egg walkers? Did they, too, have only the release of some Judge Krink, who in faraway Fourace Hill was allowed to kick and curse and bang on his tin pail? Did their judge, like mine, quickly find that even behind the walls of fantasy one had to swallow anger as neatly as, with the new table manner, one swallowed food?

When they asked, so quietly, "May we come up?" they must

surely have been really annoyed at the discovery that I had thrown a whole dressing-table set out the window, or traded my bicycle for a baseball—to name actual examples of malice and foolishness that I find in the files—but no one would know it. I sometimes wept and moved my arms as I tried to find explanations that would meet the high standards of adult logic, but it seemed that grown-ups didn't get angry, and naturally I wanted to be a grown-up. Grown-ups were free, and who didn't want to be free? So the judge folded his napkin, asked to be excused, and put his pail and shovel away as quietly as possible.

We just did make the train for Saratoga and there was a handsome admission that I was right, followed by companionable calm. There wasn't any more friction that summer, mostly because we were all too busy—Connie re-arranging the house, Pat staying out of the way, no working at the *Nutmeg* and going up to Ruth's empty Sabine Farm to let a little sunshine into the old living room where I lay on the floor and read randomly chosen books from the dusty shelves.

•   •

Heywood was busy with more important things, keeping the Newspaper Guild together, keeping the *Nutmeg* alive by borrowing money from his friends, and dealing with all the emotional shifts that were to accompany his conversion to the Catholic faith.

The Guild's left and right wings, increasingly bitter, seemed madder at each other than at the publishers, and Heywood, in the middle, sometimes seemed to the combatants to be alternately the betrayer of one side and then the other.

As much pleasure as he took out of the *Nutmeg,* the amount of money that had to be poured into it frightened him, even as the increasing stiffness of his relations with Scripps-Howard indicated that he might soon have no place left to say anything.

None of these problems, nor the fears about his health, had anything to do with the religious decision, however. The trigger had been a series of conversations at a Newspaper Guild convention with Father Edward Dowling, a lively radical who, debarred from parish duties by arthritis, had employed his energies in editing a diocesan newspaper that was a considerable headache to the hierarchy because it espoused such causes as organized labor and Loyalist Spain.

Dowling broke down the big doubt, the fear that one couldn't be a political radical and a true believer. Dowling pointed out that as a priest he was subject to a good deal more discipline than would Heywood as a communicant, which didn't keep him from rattling the collection can for his radical causes; that when the Pope spoke on religious matters he was, admittedly, the Vicar of Christ on earth, but that his political views were just those of the head of the Vatican state, a very small corner of Rome whose only colony was Castel Gandolfo, the summer Vatican. Convinced, delighted to be convinced, Heywood decided that with Dowling and Dorothy Day of the *Catholic Worker* as models he would go to Mass with all his beliefs intact and a new one added that would convince him that there was an answer to that old problem of what's on the other side of the universe, and that the answer was the Kingdom of God.

He began cautious discussions with an assortment of advisors. His lawyer, Morris Ernst, whom he had known since school days at Horace Mann, thought that on the whole it would be a good idea; Connie would in a vague way feel more comfortable, but was perfectly happy to leave the decision either way to the Commander; and Alfred McCosker, a radio executive who sometimes went to the races with Heywood, assured him that people wouldn't think the whole affair was just something to make Connie happy. McCosker sent him to Monsignor Fulton J. Sheen for instruction.

· WHOSE LITTLE BOY ARE YOU? ·

What no one seemed to have thought about was the kind of knee-jerk "No Popery" prejudice common to seventeenth-century Englishmen and twentieth-century American intellectuals. Working for Hearst would have caused much less disapproval among his friends than what they saw as joining hands with Torquemada, Savonarola, and the Borgia family, so strong in Popes and poisoners.

Protestants, Jews, Ethical Culturists, Marxists, and Atheists suddenly had one thing in common, a strong disapproval of what Heywood had done. Thousands of letters poured in and the man who had always avoided most of his mail waded grimly through the waves of condemnation. He had thought he had won a trust in his integrity and saw the trust melting with terrifying speed even among those who ought to have known him well enough to know better.

One person who might have given him strong support from the beginning and who understood and sympathized totally without any iron of shared faith in the fire was me, but I was ignorant of the whole business until a college classmate approached me waving a copy of *Time* and announced, "Hey, Woodie, did you know that your father just joined the Catholic church?"

I pretended to the knowledge just as later I pretended to knowledge of Ruth's affair with the politician, and in Heywood's case, I wasn't surprised or shocked. I had known something was in the wind when Heywood, a couple of years earlier, had stolen my Bible. This act was a little more innocent than it sounds so baldly if accurately described.

Ruth had given me the Bible, a handsome big one bound in blue leather. I was instructed sternly to pay attention to the King James English and be ready with healthy skepticism when I came to Jonah and the Whale, Joshua and the Walls, and all those miracles in the New Testament.

At one point in early adolescent pain, the kind that seems

silly when remembered but aches anyway, I whispered to a deity that I hoped could hear things Ruth and Heywood couldn't that I would read it all the way through Begats, architectural details of the Ark of the Covenant and all, in the hope that this act of piety would persuade him to ease of commitment. Heywood preferred the borrowed Word to one that, through the act of purchase, took him a step further than he was then willing to go.

I tried from time to time thereafter to get my Bible back, and even went so far as to buy him one bound in slabs of olive wood from the Holy Land, but it was too late. The familiar feel and look of the book Ruth had intended for the elevation of my language had become too precious to him, and the bookmarks multiplied among the pages.

The Broun case was still being widely and largely disapprovingly discussed when I got back from school and I prepared to enlist under his banner only to discover that as he had been afraid to tell me, so he was afraid to ask me, and that I was afraid of a rebuff as he was.

When he and Connie and Pat went to Mass there was a great tiptoeing about so as not to wake me, and I, often wakened by the sibilance of their stealth, felt that some remark, like "Have a good time" was not exactly the right one.

Our eventual discussion numbered less than twenty words. Heywood came into the living room in Stamford and said rather gruffly, "I'd like you to read this."

"This" was a piece he had written for *The New Republic* that was headed "Not in This Issue." After he handed it to me, he left the room.

I have received a number of letters and a few have been printed elsewhere in which I am asked to write an explanation of the reasons why I have become a Catholic. I have no intention of complying in this issue.

In part it is my feeling that no man should discuss those things which are closest to him without taking great care to express himself as well as his best potentialities permit. And again I bridle, for the moment at least, because most of the missives appear to come from those who seem quite ready to condemn with an answer or without. Indeed they seem to ask not so much for a statement of belief as an immediate apology.

My impulse at this point, unwisely repressed, was to stop reading and just run to wherever he was lurking and give him the mindless comfort of a hug.

"Some morning," he said later in the piece, "there will come to me a feeling that the time has come and the words will spring up in such a way that what I want to say will be done with some measure of eloquence and dignity. A merely peevish answer to a peevish communication would be of little service. I did not make any impulsive decision. I will not make any impulsive answer."

When Heywood came back into the room I handed him his typescript and with a gruffness to equal his, muttered, "It couldn't have been said better."

His sentence and mine were the only words we spoke on a subject that has filled endless volumes and hours of discussion. The best that can be said for our exchange was that unlike most religious discussions, it made its point without waste of words.

The largely hostile curiosity that battered at him then seems undiminished in those who remember him, and I have grown wearily accustomed to strangers who begin "Do you mind if I ask you a personal question?" a question that turns out not to be personal to me at all but a request for an explanation of Heywood's conversion.

He had shown his deeply religious feelings in a whole series of Christmas columns, but readers chose to view these pieces as merely picturesque. At Christmas, after all, the most vigorous unbelievers are as warmed by singing "The First Noel," and other accounts of a Savior's birth as they are by the eggnog that accompanies the singing.

Much of the piece in *The New Republic* concerned itself with Heywood's objections to the special set of rules that are supposed to apply to "public figures," those who presumably owe explanations to the providers of their fame.

One of the rules, unhappily, seems to be that the public figure must conform to the image his idolaters have constructed. The shaggy radical had no place amongst *them,* the kneelers, the mumblers of Latin, the political reactionaries.

Heywood himself had once written that, "There is not a single New York editor who does not live in mortal terror of this group," and had shared most of the liberal concerns about the crushing power of the big flat foot of Rome.

Father Dowling had swept all this away and had opened a door through which Heywood could gain the comforts of faith. I thought of Heywood when I read in the work of an old English novelist, George A. Lawrence, about the isolation that "has made many men famous by forcing them out into the world and shutting the door behind them."

Heywood gave a lot of people the illusion of intimacy and lots of them have told me about the intentness with which he listened to their troubles and the comfort he gave them, but I don't remember his saying such things about anyone.

He chose to speak of the troubles that he made up, the phobias about silly things like elevators and automobiles, because he couldn't talk about or face the aloneness that is limitless and endless.

Of course he created the problems, and maybe he made up the answer, but he got much comfort from it. He hung on to all his principles as well, as tenaciously as he hung on to my Bible (it disappeared mysteriously after his death). Although

• WHOSE LITTLE BOY ARE YOU? •

I am polite and patient with those who are still curious about his decision, I thought it made every kind of sense and wish I had said more than my single sentence of support. I know, however, that before I had gotten very far he would have been on his way to the kitchen prepared to cook up a honey-and-asparagus omelette so that egg-cracking and mess-muddling would bring the conversation to a close.

Even as the church was opening its doors, his profession seemed to be closing its. It is only speculation to say that the Guild was going to pick another president, although I believe the people who told me so, and I'm afraid Heywood did too.

There was no doubt about his rejection from the employer's end, however, and when Scripps-Howard, as fake in its liberalism as the *World* had been, declined to renew his contract, there was suddenly a nationwide lack of interest in the work of a man who was supposed to add fifty thousand readers to the circulation of any metropolitan newspaper that hired him. I am sure that his work for the Guild was the reason.

His colds and grippes became heavier and more frequent and at the height of almost every one I was, if in the neighborhood, summoned to his bedside and instructed about how to handle the many details that would follow his end.

His other companion on some of these occasions was the brilliant and unhappily honest doctor who had first shown up when four years earlier it had once again seemed likely that my end was near.

Puffy-eyed, yellow-faced, and bleeding from the nose, I had been playing a game superficially different from Heywood's, but at base as hysterically hypochondrical. I was just fine, I announced, as I groaned and oozed gore, and would be better still if some kind person would get some flannel plasters from the drugstore to ease my rheumatic pains.

My request was ignored and a summons brought the doctor, who looked at me, put a thermometer in my mouth, and improving on the first physician to doubt my staying powers, pulled Heywood out in the hall to tell him "Your son has acute Bright's disease."

Heywood's handling of this crisis was wonderfully characteristic. He arranged for me to be moved at once to a hospital room outstanding in comfort, in a hospital outstanding in its available skills. Since I couldn't get out of bed, I took the river view on faith, but visitors said it was lovely—visitors who rarely included Heywood. He showed up for two quick hellos in the forty-two days I spent there. He was so visibly afraid I was glad to see him go—still, I was sorry when he didn't return.

At his expense, however, experts in the field of the kidney passed through my room in a learned and costly parade, the whole distinguished lot of them under the supervision of a world-renowned specialist after whom a wing of the hospital has since been named.

It appears that along with the back and forth of child-psychology approaches, there are backs and forths in physiological approaches to child ailments. I am of the generation whose parents were advised to keep the tonsils intact, twin turrets of protection that were to stop harmful things from passing down the little red lane to the breadbasket—to put it in layman's terms.

It appeared, however, that a fifth column had occupied my twin turrets and that my disease was due to the fact that from these alien strongholds germs had been marching all through me for years, perhaps back to the day when I had first been despaired of.

A great specialist in tonsils was summoned to remove mine with what appeared from postoperative sensation to have been a mason's trowel, and weak but well, I was discharged in a month from the hospital.

Heywood, his fears now under control, was wonderfully

attentive and took me to Florida for convalescence. It was off-season in those days when there were seasons, and we were almost the only guests in the luxurious old Miami Biltmore Hotel. We lounged around the pool talking politics and comic strips before going to the races at Tropical Park, a little track run by Big Bill Dwyer, a hospitable man who had his friends to breakfast on a porch overlooking the finish line. Dwyer was rumored to have extensive connections with the underworld, but as one who has eaten his bacon and eggs on sunny mornings that I had been by no means certain I would ever see, I prefer to think of him as a host beyond reproach.

One can't help thinking of prissy young Queen Victoria inveighing against the excesses of her wicked uncles to Lord Melbourne, only to have that worldly old statesman reply, "But Madame, they were such jolly men."

If Heywood and I are to get together in one of those dreams, I think Bill Dwyer's porch would be a good place and I'm going to suggest it.

Back in school, I continued to mend and Heywood was the one who saw more and more of our doctor. This unsmiling man poked and prodded Heywood and pronounced him in poor shape. He prescribed dull foods in small amounts and an absolute ban on alcohol. Moderate exercise was to be taken regularly, some of it at a distressingly early hour. I think the doctor managed a thin puritanical smile at this point—and in general Heywood was to live such a life as he had never lived before, a life whose only lure was that it promised to be respectably long.

The brilliant doctor was a better internist than he was a psychologist. His story, although clinically accurate, was so stark that there was nothing for someone like Heywood to do except deny it. Shivers of his own creation were like the controlled touches of a tongue on a sore tooth, little explorations of the edges of mortality, self-guided tours that gave the illusion that one was *facing things.* Bad news was to be shut away. Fortunately or unfortunately the grim doctor went on a vacation at this point—probably two weeks of hiking over rocks—and turned his practice over to a jolly colleague who, when asked by Heywood whether sudden abstinence from alcohol was not a shock to the system, answered the question by inquiring if there was any drink in the house that they could share. He got the job of regular medical attendant somewhere between the second and third drink.

This man was spiritual brother to Heywood's dentist, a Socialist poet who could always be persuaded to put down his mirror and examination pick so that he might read an ode to Daniel de Leon which would fill up the appointment time if not Heywood's teeth. Heywood used to say that he was loyal because although the poetry was bad, it beat tooth drilling and that there was the additional comfort that whether toothache caught up with him on a tramp steamer or a tropical island, the makeshift work available there would not be inferior to what he could get at home.

This kind of thing eventually led to a lot of tooth loss and a temporary upper plate that he was to wear until a properly fitting permanent one could be made. He never went back for the final product which explains all those photos in which he is shown with a forefinger thoughtfully pressed against his incisors. He was keeping them in.

I tell the story not to mock his infirmities but to sympathize. It always has to be said again and again of Heywood that no man afraid of so many things ever accomplished so much.

Few people as frightened as he kept their idealism and their optimism so shining and unscratched.

On his fifty-first and last birthday he wrote, "I have more faith than I ever had before. People are better than I thought they were going to be—myself included. In mere physical exertion there may be some let-up. Instead of the daily constitutional of a hundred yards it will be twenty-five from now on. But at fifty-one I'm a better fighter than at twenty-one."

The whimsical remark about exercise was, oddly, quite untrue. The only advice he had taken from his brief association with the reformist physician was the business about moderate exertion at regular hours.

Golf was the game at which he had been best when young, and born before the age of the golf cart, he had to be ingenious. On his country walks he carried a seven iron, ostensibly to beat off hostile dogs but actually to practice his swing on burdock leaves and thistle heads.

When we were in Florida for one of the major hurricanes of the thirties, he got me out on the course with a bucket of practice balls and a couple of nine irons with which we lofted shots that the wind gripped as a runaway horse bites down on a bit, and carried, careering away, down the course.

"You'll never get distance like this again," cried a suddenly fearless Heywood as we fought to keep our feet so that we should not join the palm branches that were beginning to break loose and fan the air above our heads.

More prosaically, he built a pitch-and-putt course around the house in Stamford. It had every hazard except those provided by distance. There were pitches over telephone wires, special penalties for dropping into flower beds, minidrives which if long or short were subject to bounces off rocks, and little sand greens with tin can cups. All told the course had nine tees and three greens and easy access to the nineteenth hole from any place on the course.

Playing this course with Heywood I discovered a previously unknown side of him. He was a fierce competitor who took defeat with a grim determination that it should be reversed as soon as possible.

He held on to the perpetual challenge trophy, a gold-type cup won by the chorus of *Shoot the Works* in a *Daily News* long-driving contest—with great firmness, filling it with champagne after each victory over guests who were forced out onto the course whether they played golf or not.

A woman photographer, who unfortunately played very well, beat him one weekend and found a series of mysterious accidents to the car, losses of timetables, and other mishaps calculated to keep her a prisoner prolonged the visit until late in the following week. At last she had sense enough to suffer a diminution of skills and the loss of the cup to the relentless home pro. She left on the next train.

I had no such problems because in two years of trying I never beat Heywood. I pressed him closely on occasion, but when I did, I realized that conversation and geniality withered while his face, normally soft and sensitive, hardened into a sort of mask, a mixture of hunting animal and chess master. About the time that happened my game fell apart and soon we were in search of champagne—always to be opened with the neck aimed at a large frying pan whose mellow boom when cork-struck signaled another win for the perpetual holder of the perpetual challenge trophy.

After a match in which we arrived at the sixty-seventh of seventy-two holes all even, a match he then won three up and two to go, I announced my retirement from golf. I said I didn't relish the regularity of my beatings and whether it was for some reason based on Freud or a simple failure to keep my eye on the ball, I knew I was the loser and didn't like it.

Heywood moped so much over this decision that I shortly returned to the competition, secretly hoping that he might let me win one just to ginger up my enthusiasm for the game, but gripped by the concentration that had made his father a champion at so many delicate games of hand and eye, he went right back to beating me. I went off to college that fall without having drunk anything from the cup that wasn't bitter with the bubbles of defeat.

• W H O S E   L I T T L E   B O Y   A R E   Y O U ? •

Nearing the end of his newspaper contract, he had made an arrangement to join the New York *Post,* but it was at a humiliating cut in salary, and when I saw him on weekends, he seemed tired. The zest of his idealism was unflagging, but he had pounded his typewriter keys for a very long time and it was natural to hope that the new world that he was still sure was on its way, would come soon.

The weariness didn't cease, however, and I was summoned home in early December to find Heywood in the hospital. A cold had developed into the flu and then proceeded to pneumonia. He was in an oxygen tent.

I sat in the hospital waiting room all through one day as medical personnel shuttled in and out of the room. It all seemed so busy and professional that I was afraid to ask whether I could visit him, and maybe I was afraid that my visit would be declined, and maybe I was afraid to see him as he would look when the jolly joke-telling death of his playlet was waiting invisibly in the hall ready with the last and best funny story.

At evening when we were all sent home, Al Barach, once Heywood's psychiatrist and now attending him in his role as a pulmonary specialist, took me aside and said, "You're a betting man, Woodie, so you'll understand if I put the situation in racetrack terms. Heywood has about an eight-to-five chance to recover. That's not a bad bet."

I didn't tell him that Heywood had taught me not to have much faith in odds-on favorites, but somewhat comforted I went back to the friend's apartment where I was staying, only to be wakened early the next morning and told that there wasn't much more time. I remember seeing the scarlet sky of a cold dawn out the cab window and endlessly, mindlessly, forebodingly repeating under my breath an old rhyme I had learned from Ruth, "Red sky at night, sailor's delight, red sky at morning, sailor take warning." The rhyme kept me from thinking, but when I got to the hospital and found Irving there and Connie and Monsignor Sheen, I knew Heywood wasn't going to share the sailor's delight in any future flaming evening.

The shufflings in and out of the sickroom seemed faster. Connie went and then the Monsignor and then lots of people in the long white coats that reassure us at the best of times and frighten us at the worst—and suddenly someone was telling me that Heywood was dead, just as four years before it had been Heywood's voice on the telephone telling me that Ruth was dead.

Word reached me thirdhand that close to Heywood's last words had been the statement that Ring Lardner would have lived longer if he had written what he really wanted to and that Heywood, if he survived, would write about horse racing, nightclubs, gambling, and "life."

At first the two remarks seem not to make much sense, Lardner having written a wide variety of first-rate stuff—if there was something he didn't do, it was probably something impractically philosophical, the kind of thing writers dream about when posterity is winking and beckoning.

Lardner and Heywood did share, I think, a kind of painful romanticism, in Lardner's case nourished in the Penrod Schofield atmosphere of Niles, Michigan, and in Broun's, the glittering New York of Richard Harding Davis' Van Bibber. When "Lilacs" at last became "Rube," I'm sure he wanted to right wrongs as elegantly as Van Bibber had, always without getting any manure on his patent leather evening shoes.

Vulnerable in their dreaminess both men discovered a real world that was sometimes cruelly far from Tarkington's town or Davis' bright city. Lardner portrayed it with the unsparing eye of the disappointed, and Broun tried to change it.

Neither one seemed a man to end as a comfy clubby ancient, but both wrote, I think, what they wanted to and had to.

Heywood in embracing the idea of becoming a sort of Broad-

way columnist, in the company of such as O. O. McIntyre and
Mark Hellinger, was simply showing a terrible weariness. Perhaps for a moment he wanted to pull the ghost of Lardner
along into comfy clubby writing, but it seems as if each had
come, as Ruth had, to the place foretold in the picture of the
old Indian, the place where one is ready to lie down in regret-
less sleep.

The man who had so recently proclaimed that his faith had
grown with his years could hardly have been happy table-
hopping toward his typewriter, but it must have been a sadly
winning fantasy as the seams of his heart gave way.

Irving and I put our arms around each other and wept, and
I had no time then, in the middle of desolation, to wonder why
I had not had a chance for a farewell. Later I speculated about
this a great deal and wondered whether I was too far down on
a list, a list cut short by the literal bursting of Heywood's heart.
I would get distracted from speculating as to where I stood on
the list by the rich unhappy humor of the fact that the psychiatrist who had assigned Heywood's fears of heart trouble to the
realm of the hysterical had been present when the patient's
fears had proved to be totally and tragically rational. Was this
the last best joke of the man in the loud suit? Did Heywood
laugh, or did he reproach the doctor for the hours he spent
talking about his early relationships with his parents, his first
sexual fears, his problems with toilet training, and all the stuff
that goes into the search for the roots of phobias.

I didn't see Dr. Barach to ask him about this, and thirty years
later when I went to see him in the course of my own therapy
to pick up a few facts about Heywood to go with my speculations about my early parent-child relationships and the difficulties of my toilet training, it seemed tasteless to ask—or was
I afraid that my now richly embroidered fantasies about that
last conversation were more satisfying than any revelation Barach could give me?

Harry Guggenheim and his wife Alicia took Connie, Pat, and

me into their home for the days before the funeral, and we busied ourselves with the elaborate arrangements that are suitable to the departure of the notable. Saint Patrick's Cathedral was full for the funeral, most of those there having met him in that best of ways, through reading the column, that wonderful projection of intimacy and concern that shy, fat "Rube" Broun had hit on long before and developed as perhaps no one else ever did into a means of getting close to people and affecting their lives, without letting them affect his. Only in the massive protest against his conversion did his host of faceless friends ever get through to talk back to him and it hurt and shook him badly.

I doubt that most of the mourners at that funeral were very happy with Monsignor Sheen's eulogy which seemed to say that Heywood had not done much of anything until he made the important decision to seek grace. When Connie and I got into the car with Sheen and Quentin Reynolds for the rainy day drive—Why is it always a rainy day?—to Gates of Heaven Cemetery, I braced myself for the difficult task of being polite enough to Sheen so that Connie should not be upset, and chilly enough so that Sheen should know how much I disapproved of a speech that left out almost half a century of dedicated life.

The monsignor shot down this complex scheme before the oily clunk of the limousine door had reached our ears. He entered into an easy chat with me about prospects for the coming baseball season, a subject about which politeness is unnecessary and chilliness silly. I am sorry to say that we got on famously and as to my demonstration of disapproval, I am sure that he had sensed it as we crossed the sidewalk and that, worse still, he had forgiven it.

Pegler, in the attack on Reynolds that led to a libel suit, alleged among other things that Quent had suggested marriage to Connie during this ride to the cemetery. The idea of a proposal filtering through an intervening discussion of the weaknesses of the Brooklyn infield is, God knows, funny, but the reason I wasn't called on during the suit as a witness is rather sad.

I was summoned to a preliminary meeting with Quent's lawyer, Louis Nizer, who got right down to the matters on which he wished my reassurance.

"Pegler claimed," he said in the richly horrified voice of a professional reciter at the climax of "The Face on the Barroom Floor," "that in your country home there were sexual incidents involving blacks and whites."

I laughed reassuringly. "He must mean Paul Robeson."

Nizer staggered back like someone who has stumbled over the derelict hero of the poem.

"You see," I went on, "Paul was wonderfully attractive and it wouldn't surprise any sensible person if there had been some knocking at his bedroom door. I mean, if you had met him you would understand—"

"Thank you," said Nizer, and went on to the next sinful point. "He says there was mixed nude bathing in the lake behind your house."

He said it as if the bathers were in the water as a mere refreshing interlude between the exercise of assorted vices, and I realized how hopeless was my task even as I tried.

"It was the twenties, Mr. Nizer! Don't you remember the twenties? All that social protest, all that outcry against something called Grundyism? To tell you the truth it was rather sad to see them, all protesting their freedom through nudity and all wishing that, the protest made, they could get back into their bathing suits."

Louis Nizer was unimpressed by my argument and I never saw him again until long after the trial when I protested mildly that his best-seller, *My Life in Court* (I guess that's where he spent the twenties) had repeated some of the libels against Heywood. He claimed Reynolds' success in the law suit was, in itself, a satisfactory refutation. He wasn't much impressed by my protest that time either.

•   •

When the business of the burial was over my first thought was to get home and be at last alone with my bewilderment and unhappiness. The first problem was where was home and the second, why did I want to be alone?

I solved the first problem as I so often had, by going to a friend's house, a big rambling place on the Palisades that had taken me in so often that a packed suitcase sat there at all times to mark out a corner that was considered mine.

The second problem I was not to solve for many years. At the time it just seemed to me important to pull together as many memories as possible of Heywood and Ruth, and that this would best be done without the distraction of company. What I wanted to do, I guess, was to set up a house inside my head where they could go on living, a place with three floors and a basement, one floor for each of us and a basement where we could all get together. Everything I remembered would help to furnish the place and give it life, color, and continuity.

We had all made a big effort at independence and in our different ways had failed, and here we could finally talk it over.

Of course, I didn't think of the house idea then, in the days after my return to school, or for many years more. It didn't matter. The house took shape and we took our places in it.

It is at least ten years since I stopped having the dream that I alone of the soldiers in World War II had been kept in the army. In the dream I pled with assorted officers for some consideration but they always said, "We need you, Sergeant," and I sighed and saluted. I used to think this was part of some fear of being taken back after 1945, but as the years passed and I ceased to be a prospect even for the Home Guard, it became clear that some other anxiety was marching around in my uniform.

Well, it seems that the army camp was Eighty-fifth Street and that resentfully but relentlessly I wanted to get back there, to those unsatisfactory officers, Ruth and Heywood, who paid me the compliment, at least in my dreams, of needing me.

If we make up our own dreams, why don't I make Heywood say "333 West 85th Street," when I ask for the address that he never gives? I wonder, too, why Ruth appears so much less often in those shadow reunions. In her case I think it is because even now I am afraid of the questions that might be asked— questions about how I failed her, questions that still murmur around the back of my mind even when I'm awake, questions I'm likely to put into terrifying forms when guilt comes out of its cubbyhole under the stairs.

Heywood's place in the dreams is different because in the end he left me and so still won't say where he is. We both look forward to getting together—someday—which is just how it was in those years when he kept me at his side in Florida or called me from school to join him in a nightclub, both of us talking away about comics and racing and politics and hoping for the Gee-Dad-Hey-Son moments, real getting together, which never quite happened.

It's too late to ask but I do sometimes wonder what Heywood's other drinking companions thought about the solemn, silent—if they were lucky—little boy sitting behind his bottle of "Canadian" beer in Tony's, where Heywood looked down at himself from a caricature mural; in Jack and Charlie's, as "21" was called in the days when the red and white tablecloths weren't chic but just something that could be cheaply replaced if ripped up in a raid; or in the Stork Club, which was cozy and unfashionable on the second floor of a brownstone.

Among schoolmates and, unfortunately, teachers, I had a totally undeserved reputation for a kind of weary sophistication. I was supposed to be the preppy J. K. Huysmans, but in fact the weariness was only fear and my supposed "wickedness" was pretty much limited to the lurid nature of my ill-informed erotic fantasies, fantasies I was much too timid to drag into the world of real life.

I remember once an actor with a young face and old eyes telling me about an organization that kept files on the oddest of desires.

"They match you up in their card catalogues with someone who likes the same thing," he murmured. "And then they send you to a farm in upstate New York where you Do It." I suppose that's what my disapproving teachers meant by sophistication, but I didn't want a place in the file.

Child rearing used to be just a matter of keeping them alive until they were old enough to get outside with a hoe, but it has become, as we all know, a difficult business, and my parents were in the first generation that really got psychological about it.

My present friends point out that I don't really have any kick coming about my odd "little-grown up" upbringing because I pass all the tests. I have been married but once and am happy in that marriage. I have a son with whom, I think, I get on very well. I may have been a long time getting there, but I am, in worldly terms, a success. I have given up smoking, don't drink all that much, and all in all seem a credit to what for lack of a better word we'll call "The System."

There is perhaps a kind of irony in the little boy who was expected to be an instant grown up but was still dreaming in his fifties of returning to a puzzling parental authority in a symbolic army camp.

There are a lot of other ironies, but if ironies are the worst of your burdens you can give yourself a cautious pat on the back and say that you're okay so far.

Old John Wright, the horse trainer, was much quicker getting out of his boxcar than I was in shutting behind me the door of the house where I almost died and where I was often not sure I deserved to live. Still we both made it, and when I came down from my room the second time, leaving dreams behind and the self-concerned life that was my bulwark against the burdens of a difficult life, it was much more peaceful.

I'm glad they don't have to go upstairs anymore to discuss what I've been doing. I hope they are, too.